CONQUEROR MINDSET

CONQUER THE MONSTER

Robert Conqueror Roberts

ISBN 979-8-88616-965-2 (paperback)
ISBN 979-8-88616-966-9 (digital)

Christian Faith Publishing
832 Park Avenue
Meadville, PA 16335
www.christianfaithpublishing.com

Printed in the United States of America

INTRODUCTION

In life, we are going to run into situations and circumstances that may seem to be beyond our control and understanding. These circumstances and situations may try to make us feel overwhelmed or full of self-doubt, guilt, anxiety, insecurity, stress, and fear. We have the power to change our current circumstances and manifest greatness in our lives. Fear comes in many forms. Fear can come in the form of the fear of change, rejection, phobias, loneliness, public speaking, heights, animals, insects, panic disorders, failure, loss, intimacy, being judged, success, and the unknown just to name a few. Every fear affects every person differently.

We may face circumstances and situations from our past, present, or foreseeable future that may try to make us feel overwhelmed, full of self-doubt, stress, depression, resistance, insecurity, sadness, anger, and anxiety. We have the power to change our current circumstances and manifest greatness in our lives.

When we face stimuli that may be new, uncomfortable, or unknown, some people tend to view this phenomenon as fear, when it may be a multitude of other emotions, depending on the lens we choose to look through.

This is an important guide that is based on the principles that can lead to one's success in every aspect of their life. This guide holds the blueprint that will assist you in overcoming and conquering stumbling blocks that may have been holding you back from being your very best.

Having a conqueror mindset allows us to attain mindfulness and a better sense of awareness as we learn who we really are.

By having a conqueror mindset, we will understand that the mind, body, and spirit are interconnected. As we obtain a conqueror mindset, we will better understand that everything in life is based on our perception and our perspective, as well as the position and angle in which we choose to view ourselves. The lens in which we choose to view ourselves then influences the way in which we view others, stimuli, and the world around us.

After we attain a conqueror mindset, we will discover the blueprint that will allow us to identify, overcome, and conquer stress, fear, unforgiveness, addiction, anxiety, childhood trauma, anger, and negativity in our lives. This will allow us to feel renewed and have sustainable energy. It enables us to be the light in a roomful of darkness.

We must remember that energy cannot be created or destroyed, but it can only be transferred from one object to another. Sometimes in our life, we have to dig in deep and encourage ourselves, knowing that words are powerful especially if backed with action. We have to continue to realize that every day is a battle, and we need to walk in the confidence knowing that we have already won. By having a conqueror mindset, we will have a battle plan that will allow us to walk through life stress-free, in love, and full of expectancy.

By having a conqueror mindset, we will have a battle plan that will allow us to take action which is in direct opposition to fear. As we obtain a conqueror mindset, we will have the ability and self-awareness to walk through life stress-free, in love, and full of expectancy.

As a conqueror, we will achieve a state of mindfulness as we walk in humility and with confidence knowing that no weapon, obstacle, or monster that we may face can defeat us. A conqueror mindset teaches us that we already have victory, and all we have to do is have faith, believe, and take action. It is time for us to plow our field, plant our seed in life, and prepare for rain. If we do this, in due season, we will have a harvest that will produce beautiful fruit. We have to continue to be quick to listen, slow to speak, and bold as a lion as we walk in love and conquer the monster of fear. It is time for us to step outside of our comfort zone. It is time for us to let go of fear and embrace freedom.

CHAPTER 1

IDENTIFY THE MONSTER

On a dark rainy night, while walking down a long, poorly lit hallway in a maximum-security detention unit, I observed large steel cell doors to the left and right of me. I could see menacing eyes glaring at me through the small, reinforced windows at the front of each door. It was so eerily quiet that you could hear a pin drop.

Suddenly, I could hear what sounded like thunder off in the distance. I walked farther down the hallway with four large men dressed in all-black tactical gear with helmets and less-lethal equipment, such as stun shields, batons, gas irritants, and the like. It was time for us to conduct a use of force for a noncompliant and extremely violent murderer that was nicknamed "The Monster."

I had years of experience in law enforcement, corrections, intelligence units, fugitive task force units, special operations teams, and hand-to-hand combat; but as a new member of this tactical and emergency response team, I wanted to hear and fully understand what the threat was that I was about to face.

Prior to this mission, I was briefed and informed that the inmate was serving several consecutive life sentences for gruesome offenses. I was told that he was enormous, relentless, and extremely violent and that no one was ever able to successfully record his height and most recent weight because the inmate simply refused.

I was informed that the Monster, just twenty minutes earlier, violently assaulted a nurse that was distributing medication on the unit by striking her in the face with a biological weapon, which was referred to in this maximum-security unit as a glass poop bomb.

This destructive weapon was a mixture of human feces, urine, and crushed-up glass that came from lightbulbs that were taken out of a light fixture that was in the inmate's cell.

By using the human feces, urine, and crushed glass, the tiny pieces of glass operated similar to razor-sharp shrapnel.

This weapon was designed to be thrown in a person's face, and because of the shock and pungent odor, it would cause a person to react by wiping their eyes and face vigorously in an attempt to be able to see and breathe.

Unfortunately, if a person tried to clear their eyes, mouth, or their face from this sticky substance by wiping it off, the glass-filled feces and urine would then tear deep into a person's eyes and flesh, causing them to receive infections and diseases, along with permanent scarring and possible blindness.

Counselors, nurses, psychologists, chaplains, and supervisors tried to de-escalate the situation to no avail. All negotiations were unsuccessful.

After this vicious assault, the monster informed the prison supervisors that he was armed with a homemade prison knife, or what is referred to as a shank, and stated that he was going to kill himself as well as any staff member that approached his now-barricaded cell. I was informed that the Monster was also naked, covering himself in baby oil and human waste. He booby-trapped his cell, and he made statements, saying, "Bring on the goon squad." After pouring baby oil and lotion on the floor, he flooded his sink, as well as his toilet filled with days-old human waste. The Monster had a wet T-shirt wrapped around his head as a homemade gasmask and filter as he was prepared for us to follow that textbook procedure of deploying gas, pepper spray, and other chemical irritants.

This inmate that called himself The Monster had spent more years locked up behind bars than as a free man. He had vast knowledge and experience of various levels of combat and tactics in numerous prison systems throughout the country. For his personal entertainment, the Monster would commit horrific and extremely disturbing acts of violence against unsuspecting staff members and offenders just so that he could face the prison or detention centers' tactical teams. The Monster found pleasure in sending staff members to the emergency room with life-threatening injuries just so that he could test and face the emergency response teams at whatever prison or detention center that he was transferred to. The Monster referred to each physical encounter with special response teams as getting in reck. The Monster's custody classification was at the highest security threat level. He would conduct planned and spontaneous attacks on staff members or inmates without warning and without justification. He found joy in causing others pain. Some government and private agencies would pay other agencies to house the Monster.

He was assaultive and could make a weapon out of anything. He was known for altering items and being in possession of padlocks in socks, sharpened razors melted down into toothbrushes, broken air vents and bedsprings made into makeshift knives, paper hardened with toothpaste and sharpened, soap in socks, battery acid, and the like.

The monster was familiar with the rules of engagement. He had been incarcerated off and on since he was a juvenile. He studied and knew every type of local, state, regional, and federal policy; use of force continuum, standard operating procedure, and tactic that was authorized and unauthorized. He knew that by violently assaulting staff, destroying government property, and threatening to kill himself, they would, according to policy, require us to restrain him and transport him to a suicide-watch unit for his safety and the safety of staff members. This inmate was so frightening that inmates and staff members would provide him with sensitive information out of fear.

The Monster was observant, vigilant, and calculated. If a staff member walked by his cell, the Monster could tell who the staff member was even from a distance, without fully seeing their face. This Monster would tell the staff member what type of car they drove to work and what happened in roll call meetings before the shift. We had to have key covers affixed on our prison, Folger Adam keys, because the Monster memorized which key went to what door. The Monster was so sophisticated that he could send unauthorized inmate-to-inmate notes and prison messages called kites by using strings that were torn from altered bedsheets, referred to as fishing lines, from cell to cell, as well as through the plumbing and air-conditioning vents to other inmates that were in cells on other floors in the prison. On several occasions, the Monster would tell staff members what car they drove to work and what their small children's names were, and which schools they went to. These types of tactics scared some people, and they suddenly felt overcome by fear, stress, and anxiety.

Because of his vast knowledge and love for confusion, anarchy, and destruction, he was extremely dangerous.

This Monster was very large and highly intelligent. He understood how to manipulate, intimidate, and simply frighten prison officials and leadership, their staff, and other inmates.

If a person dare slipped, missed a security check, made a mistake, took a shortcut, or went over the line in order to gain control, the Monster would pounce on the opportunity to use every loophole or policy and procedure to create a trap for the staff member or opposing inmate. The Monster would file grievances, false claims, and accusations against staff members to create confusion, distractions, and chaos.

For example, when he wanted an extra food tray, he would eat the majority of his food and, soon after, rip off his pubic hairs and sprinkle them on his tray, stating foul play. Staff members consistently backed down and refused to challenge him, afraid that the inmate would file more false complaints and state that his rights were being violated. The Monster continually assaulted staff members but screamed victim when it suited his agenda.

In every prison and detention facility that the Monster transferred to, the administration, staff, and other inmates found themselves overwhelmed by the Monster. He understood the system and how to utilize it for his benefit.

The Monster knew how to push staff members' buttons and get them to become so distracted that they would get discouraged or so upset that it would cause them to lose their confidence, integrity, composure, bearing, professionalism, and purpose, which led them to make mistakes that would cost them their peace, positive reputation, livelihood, freedom, or their life. He knew how to manipulate people and had a history of pitting inmates against inmates and staff against staff. If a staff member came in to work with a smile and in good spirits, the Monster would ensure that they left with a frown and in a negative state of mind.

Even though the Monster never took a shower, he somehow sweet-talked female staff members into making mistakes that cost them their career, reputation, dignity, and their freedom.

The Monster caused some staff members to be so bothered that they would show up to work late or become so exhausted after leaving work they would get into car wrecks on the way home. Some staff members that had encounters with the Monster over time, because of the stress, sometimes had thoughts of harming themselves and others. The Monster affected people directly and indirectly. Because of the Monster, some people tried to mask their feelings, so they became consumed with work that they would find themselves becoming irritable and neglecting their priorities at home.

The Monster seemed to enjoy making such a negative impact on people that it would affect their interactions with others in a harmful way. Some staff members developed mental, emotional, and physical health problems because of the stress that the Monster caused. He affected people in such a profound and negative manner that many people developed eating disorders, high blood pressure, sleeping troubles, headaches, muscle tension, nerve spasms, stomach and digestive issues, insomnia, paranoia, marital problems, depression, anxiety, irritability, migraines, body aches, anger management problems, addiction to harmful drugs, and panic attacks.

Having to interact with the Monster over time seems to cause some staff members to have low self-esteem, problems in their relationships, chronic stress, and destructive and unhealthy habit and behavior development—such as alcoholism, gambling, overeating, excessive shopping, hoarding disorders, smoking, addiction to pornography, drug abuse, and the like.

Some staff members resigned because of the Monster. Some people lost their rank, promotions, benefits, relationships, reputation, self-esteem, peace, joy, happiness, and purpose because of the Monster.

Male and female staff members were continually compromised one by one even though they were warned about this monster. The Monster seemed to know just what tactics to use for each staff member. He seemed to know what buttons to press and what bait to dangle in front of each staff member to make good people stray from what they knew was right. The Monster became whatever he needed to be to draw his victim into his trap—similar to a large poisonous spider waiting for his prey to land in his web.

It would bother other inmates and offenders being denied the opportunity to be in the general population: no phone time, no TV time, no commissary, no stamps, no visitation, no supplies, and no yard or recreational time; but this monster seemed to enjoy what other inmates would have thought was torture. The Monster thrived on his isolation and continued to run the whole prison from his cell in the segregation unit. Compromised staff and inmates would assist in sending and delivering unauthorized messages and contraband throughout the facility on the Monster's behalf.

The Monster was consistently in possession of extra mattresses, excessive uniforms, unauthorized cleaning chemicals, drugs, weapons, cigarettes, prison hooch alcohol, and cell phones. The Monster was the most isolated inmate in the prison, but he was always in possession of the most contraband. When he wanted food from fast-food restaurants, he would get the food. When he wanted the newest cell phones and electronic devices, he would receive the newest cell phones and electronic devices.

Because the Monster did not watch television or use the prison phone, the threat of that being taken away from him made it as if he had no weakness, as it related to discipline and tools of control that prison leadership could use to gain compliance. The Monster ran and controlled everything from his cell including, but not limited to, all gambling at the prison, inmate-on-inmate assaults, and inmate-on-staff assaults. The Monster had everything to gain in every scenario and nothing to lose. Or so it would seem.

CHAPTER 2

MAKE A BATTLE PLAN

Prior to suiting up for the cell extraction in debriefing, I was informed about an incident that occurred involving a violent use of force with the Monster a year earlier. This incident centered around a staff member who was a mental health professional and supervisor. He worked as an adjunct professor in the area. Although he was talented and highly educated, unfortunately, he was rude and arrogant, and he belittled his fellow staff members. Because of his privileged disposition, he had a habit of talking down to people instead of talking to people respectfully.

This gentleman was disrespectful and the type of person that was the reason why so many people dreaded coming in to work on a Monday morning. He would consistently send staff members that worked under him abrasive and condescending group emails, telling them to do this or to do that, but he would not have the common courtesy to say hello or good morning. He took pride and seemed to enjoy finding fault in others. He never showed grace or mercy as he sent out group emails and made comments on conference calls that he knew would belittle and embarrass others. He talked about people behind their backs and would create hostile working environments for others. He was insecure and would put his job over his own family. He was intimidated by anyone at his job that had more knowledge than him and would make things difficult for people that he felt did not fear him.

He would only reach out to staff members to correct them but never connect with them.

A conqueror mindset teaches us that in proper communication, we need to connect before we become direct. We need to become active listeners. This was the type of person where his job title and position were his identity. He would be quick to remind people what his position, education, and title were, almost as if it was a part of his name.

Some people had consistently questioned why a man who had no leadership, people skills, or ever worked with offenders was granted the title and position of supervisor over staff members and inmates. This professional was what some would refer to as a "telephone tough guy", but when in person, he interacted with most people differently. He spoke rudely to offenders that were behind cell doors and became more passive when standing face-to-face with an inmate. He put on a show at work, as he was rude and aggressive with staff members but passive and buddy-buddy with offenders.

As the story goes, the professional wanted to prove that he had the power and ability to make inmates comply with his demands. One day, after having a conversation with the Monster, he appeared to somehow convince the Monster to step out of his cell and walk down the hall to a nearby conference room.

This professional was blinded by his own desire to be recognized, to receive credit, and to be praised by others so badly that he never took the time to question if he convinced the Monster to come into the conference room, or if the Monster convinced him to take him out of his cell.

Never make a deal with the devil and always pay attention to the details. Due to the arrogance, need for acceptance, insecurity, and pride, the professional made a backdoor deal with the Monster. The professional asked the Monster to come to a nearby conference room in front of the prison leadership. Apparently, the Monster told him that he would comply, but he complained that his wrist and ankles were too large for the uncomfortable restrains and that he wanted a special diet tray, as well as ease on security restrictions, prior to going to the conference room.

Because of the professional's undue familiarity with inmates—and his infatuation and admiration for bullies, dictators, terrorists, strongmen, abusers, thugs, and tyrants—he became blinded by his own ambition to have the appearance of power that he developed tunnel vision. The mental health professional chose to ignore the Monster's prison file and security classification level. The professional did not understand that there was a difference between an inmate and a convict.

Instead of following the policy and having the Monster—who was a maximum-security high-risk offender housed in an administrative segregation unit, in four-point restraints, which consisted of handcuffs, waist chain, black box, leg irons/shackles, a stun belt, a spit mask, and at least three transport officers and a supervisor—the prideful mental health professional somehow authorized the Monster to exit his cell being handcuffed in the front with no escort. He apparently wanted to show off the Monster, almost as if he was an over-the-top animal trainer that would jump in a cage with a wild grizzly bear to get a reaction from the crowd.

The professional, in an attempt to show off the Monster like a shiny new toy, invited several staff members including counselors, psychologists, and other administrators to the conference room to have them observe him in action. Little did he know that the Monster wanted the higher-ranked brass and supervisors in that room to begin with. The Monster simply put on an acting job utilizing the weaknesses, pridefulness, insecurity, and gullibility of the mental health professional for another objective.

I was told that the hostage situation took several hours and that ungodly things happened in the room that day. Over a dozen staff members were violated, assaulted, and seriously injured that day in ways that a person who has not worked in this environment would never understand. The events that transpired that day were so egregious that to this day, that room is still sealed off and restricted to staff.

When people in the general public hear of some of the most violent and terrifying people on the planet, and they say, "Lock them in a dungeon and throw away the key," they have to remember that while they are running for their lives in fear, there are brave and courageous men and women who are running toward that danger. It takes a special person to run toward the fire, explosions, fight, carnage, and chaos. The men and women who run toward danger and take appropriate action have a conqueror mindset.

As we think of some of the most dangerous criminals in the world, we have to remember that someone has to arrest these individuals and house them in a humane manner in correctional facilities and detention centers across the world. Without first responders, there would be no response to chaos and mayhem. While the military, law enforcement, and corrections officials who do the job the right way need to be honored, recognized, and celebrated for being a blessing to others and for their courageous service, the military, law enforcement, and corrections officials who have hatred, malice, greed, and evil in their heart need to be fired and prosecuted when warranted.

CHAPTER 3

THE CALM BEFORE THE STORM

With all that backstory, we fast-forward to this present moment in time, now walking down this hallway with the clear understanding that things were going to get awfully physical.

As we approached the cell door to the Monster, we discovered that the loud thunder-like sound that we heard was not thunder at all. It was the Monster preparing for battle by violently ramming and banging his head against the wall. Staff members opened a nearby chase closet and turned off the water to the Monster's cell to stop the water from coming out of the sprinkler head, sink, and toilet, but the damage was already done. Water, baby oil, and human waste now flowed from the Monster's cell down the hall. Due to a nearby air vent, the pungent odor of days-old human waste created a septic and sewer-like stench that made our stomachs turn and eyes water.

As we arrived at the cell door, due to the vibration of the Monster banging his head on the wall, we could hear the cell door and the surrounding walls vibrating. The Monster's scare tactics worked, as I could see that most of the supervisors present became overwhelmed with fear. They also were distracted and nervous because they could not understand how a man could generate the type of force necessary to shake reinforced concrete walls and a steel door.

I will never forget one supervisor's frozen face of terror as he pointed to the floor at a large puddle of liquid that was vibrating every time the Monster slammed his head into the wall. The ripples in the water resembled a miniature version of a small rock being thrown in a pond, causing the water to ripple in waves. It also looked like a scene from a dinosaur or monster movie. The sound of the Monster yelling was similar to the roar of a lion or a bear and reverberated down the unit and hallway, that we had to use hand signals to communicate more effectively.

The inmate had previously jammed the tray slot to the cell and used his mattress and rolled-up wet blankets as an additional barrier. The Monster sealed the door in such a manner that it was seemly impossible for us to deploy gas irritants into the cell.

It was time. I observed what is referred to as a crash cart in the area. This heavy box on wheels contained the who's who of weapons, stun grenades, pepper ball grenades, stun batons, riot suppression equipment, rifles and shotguns loaded with less-lethal rounds, MK-9s, oleoresin capsicum (OC) and chlorobenzylidenemalononitrile (CS) gas, sledgehammers, extra restraints, tasers, torches, saws, and the like.

Higher-ranking heavily armed supervisors and a prison cameraman looked at us with anxious faces as if we were at the entrance of a cave to face a dragon. They began to record the entry. My team and I lined up in preparation for a type of dynamic style breaching formation, waiting for the door to be opened. With my lead officer—a tank of a man in front of me standing at 6'5", 350 pounds—holding an electric shield with over 50,000 volts of electricity, I knew that the team was ready for this tactical entry. The other team members were all approximately 6'4", 300 pounds. I was the little guy on the team standing at 6'2", roughly 225 pounds at that time.

I observed a supervisor who was our breacher. He was an incredible person and was armed with a modified less-lethal shotgun that was strapped to his back and loaded with an assortment of impact munitions. He removed a large set of Folger Adams keys from his keyholder and began to shake nervously while attempting to place the key in the cell door keyhole. I observed his hands shaking as he fumbled with the keys, trying to remove obstructions that were jammed in the lock by the Monster. After hearing the jingle of the keys, the loud banging noise stopped as the Monster waited silently.

It seemed as if the Monster was listening for the sound of the key turning. That brief moment right before breaching a door is the most intense, terrifying, or exciting experience depending on the lens you choose to look through.

As the hard plastic visor attached to my helmet began to fog up conveniently in that exact moment, with no time to wipe my face shield, I quickly noticed that the placement of the hinges on the cell doors were different from what we were told in the briefing.

We planned for a heavy steel door with hinges on the right that opened inward. I noticed that we were standing in front of a steel door with hinges on the right that opened outward. In a breaching scenario, this is a big deal. We needed to regroup and line our tactical column to the opposite side. Without breaking ranks or formation in light of the new factors and variables while still following my chain of command, I quietly informed the lead supervisor on duty who was the acting incident commander. He stated that his mind was made up and that we would stick to the plan that he designed.

We needed to make a reassessment, but because of pride, the lead supervisor refused to make the necessary change. Another secondary supervisor was in the area, and I observed him inform the lead supervisor that we would be at a tactical disadvantage if we stayed with the original plan.

I have learned that in life, if a person is prudent or wise, they must be willing to humble themselves if they were incorrect about something, while a stubborn and arrogant person will double down and soon play the fool.

Sometimes in life, we may find out that a situation may dictate a change in our course of action. As much as some people despise taking a detour, we have to remember that if we simply ignore the warning signs on the road of life, we may find ourselves on a path to destruction.

By having a conqueror mindset, we will have humility, which will allow us to have the capacity to recognize the signs and take appropriate action in real time. We will recognize that a wise person has to be willing to humble themselves and receive wise counsel.

We all may know people who are willing to sink the entire ship due to possible damage to their self-image and superficial ego. I have learned that this type of behavior sounds like pride, but it is a combination of pride, insecurity, arrogance, and fear. Sadly, there are people in life who are willing to hurt others for their own selfish ambitions. After inventing the conqueror mindset, I have discovered that every prideful person that you see or a person full of pride is a person full of fear, insecurity, and self-doubt. These people know right from wrong and truth from fiction, but they would rather hold on to a lie and live a life in fear just so that they do not have to face the ugly truth about themselves. They want to hide behind a false perception of themselves and hold on to what they feel is power, prestige, title, position, or popularity rather than look at themselves truthfully in the mirror.

These types of people are willfully blind and try to hide the fact that they are full of fear as they turn their heads and look the other way when they see wrongdoing. In an attempt to project self-confidence and self-assurance, in many cases, the monster of fear takes on the form of aggressive posturing within them. Because they are secretly struggling with their true identity and do not know who they really are, they continually seek titles, positions, and acronyms behind their name so that they can have people garner them the respect, recognition, admiration, standing, and attention that they have been seeking their whole life.

Their appetite for recognition, power, and control is never satisfied and comes from a place of insecurity. Their goal in life is to climb the ladder, but when they finally reach the top hoping to feel satisfied, they realize that they're lonely. They were so anxious about arriving at the destination at an appointed time that they did not take the time to enjoy the journey getting there.

They are driven by a wanting to be liked, respected, or feared. They are struggling with personal agendas that cause them to have self-esteem issues. They intentionally seek positions and titles in society so that they can feel a sense of power, control, and authority over another person.

In some circumstances, they were handed the position, got the promotion too early, and were not ready for the big moment as they clinch on to the proverbial chip on their shoulder that they have struggled with for years and in many cases refused to address sense childhood.

Because of pride, fear of looking weak, losing power, feeling small, or being wrong, this type of person who is struggling in their battle with fear finds difficulty in accepting advice, a suggestion, or correction. They constantly feel as if someone is out to get them or wants what they have.

They are willing to lose and selfishly destroy the reputation, livelihood, and lives of the people around them. They can direct and order someone into battle, but they are not willing to model the way, lead from the front, and join the fight. We can recognize the monster of fear in this type of person. They will try to disguise their fear by demonstrating behaviors that resemble a person who may be arrogant as they take on a characteristic of exaggerating their own abilities and importance. They try to adopt a "my way or the highway" attitude with ultimatums and conditions. They thrive on emotional abuse as they become braggadocious and at times passive aggressive. They seek admiration and control. Internally, everything is a competition as they look for opportunities to have an argument because of their appetite for conflict and the desire to be right.

When there is injustice or misconduct being committed, they usually become silent and complicit out of fear of being ostracized from the group that they seek attention and approval from. When the camera comes on or if they are in front of an audience, they become even more dangerous and all about the show. Because of their insecurity and eagerness to be recognized, they speak without thinking and later give reluctant, poorly scripted halfhearted apologies to appease others. On the outside, they appear to be strong as steel; but on the inside, they are soft as cotton.

As we know, a prudent and wise person will see danger and take refuge, but the simple keep going and pay the penalty. As we develop a conqueror mindset, we will understand that strength does not lie in the one that always gives direction; it lies in the one that can humble themselves and receive wise counsel.

This reminded me of the coach that we all know in every sport who knows he or she needs to change what they're doing because it is not working, but they stay the course and are willing to lose the game based on their false sense of a principle or a preconceived notion that is based on lack of knowledge and their own ego.

For example, the football coach who has an unstoppable running back and an amazing offensive line but will choose to pass the ball at the one-yard line in a crowd and wonder why the ball was intercepted and they lost the game.

The basketball coach would rather lose the game by keeping their favorite player on the court who is having an off night and is fatigued instead of putting in an experienced player who is on their bench who is well-rested and ready to go.

Unfortunately, because of pride, arrogance, and fear, some people who call themselves supervisors or managers will never become leaders simply because they are willing to accept losing—people getting injured or killed—rather than simply letting go of pride, humbling themselves, and admitting that they were only human and that they may have made a mistake. These types of people feel threatened by others who walk with confidence and know their value. They do not like to feel as if they are being challenged, and they do not like to hear the word *no*. So they surround themselves with yes-men and people who they feel they can control and manipulate.

As we know, a foolish and ignorant person full of pride will always be right in his own eyes. Wise people will always listen and take heed to advice.

With several supervisors and managers in one area, I could see that the lead supervisor who was the acting incident commander on the scene was a supervisor and manager, but he was not a leader. If I could see that, so could the Monster.

The lead supervisor, who was the onsite-incident commander, first tried to make a deal with the Monster by offering the Monster two extra food trays in return for his good behavior. After all that had transpired, the team and I were shocked by that gesture. The Monster knew the use of force continuum and understood that negotiations have already been attempted and failed. By knowing the rules of engagement and that the supervisor was not following protocol, the Monster knew at that moment that the incident commander was full of fear. The Monster, now feeling as if he was in control, agreed to this transaction. The supervisor then began to walk around and stare at other staff members with a smirk on his face. With his nose up, head held high, and chest out, he appeared to be in a prideful gloat.

After eating both extra food trays, the Monster laughed at the supervisor, who appeared to be celebrating prematurely. After being laughed at, the supervisor seemed to be humiliated as the Monster then began to laugh, mock, and curse the lead supervisor while going on a tirade and using profane speech in reference to what he claimed to be pubic hair in his food. Subsequently, the Monster then used those two extra food trays to resecure and fortify his cell tray slot, now making it more difficult for us to make entry.

Some supervisors and people in positions of authority often get lost behind their power, title, status, education, and position and suffer the consequences later. Hiding behind a title, status, or position will cause us to have tunnel vision as we are walking on our path in life. By having a conqueror mindset, we will remember that by a fruit, a tree is recognized and that only a good tree can produce good fruit. If a tree is producing rotten fruit, this means that the tree is rotten; but if a tree is producing fresh and healthy fruit, this means that it is coming from a good tree.

When dealing with a monster, thug, abuser, bully, tyrant, terrorist, or dictator, we cannot reason or bargain with them. If we think that we will give them what they want just to keep the peace, we will be sadly mistaken. We must remember that they are who they are.

If a monster has your country surrounded and is pointing missiles at you but tells you he is simply doing a training exercise, do not believe the monster. If a monster is pulling out his knife in front of you and gripping it firmly while staring at you, telling you to trust him, do not believe the monster's words. If a monster commits domestic violence and apologizes as he promises that he will not do it again, know your worth and your value and do not believe him. If a monster tells you that he doesn't like you and wants to harm you and later says that he was just joking or misspoke, we must remember that the words that come out of a person's mouth are an overflow of their heart and how they truly feel. So the next time someone tells you that they did not mean to say something, you must remember that they meant to say it, but they just did not mean for it to be said out loud.

The only way we can decipher what the true intentions of a monster are, is by being quick to listen and slow to speak.

Sometimes our eyes can be deceiving, but our gut feeling seldomly lies. If a monster has barricaded himself in a room after violently attacking someone, do not sit back in fear. In these moments, it is not time for us to freeze. It is time for us to develop a conqueror mindset, identify the threat, take appropriate action, and win.

If a Monster sees a sign in an area that says, "No weapons allowed," he is not going to abide by the sign. In fact, he is going to look at every person in that area as a potential unarmed target; and in his mind, he is the wolf, and they are the sheep. Monsters don't care about laws, order, or rules. As a matter of fact, they look at these rules, laws, and orders as a way to find a chink in the armor to complete their true objective, which is to kill, steal, and destroy. They don't care about institutional or international rules, norms, or laws. They look to exploit, intimidate, and destroy any sense of reality or normalcy that others may hold dear or sacred.

In this intense moment, instead of giving the Monster loud, direct, and strong verbal orders and commands, the lead supervisor simply requested and asked the Monster, in a very timid and quiet voice, to stop his actions, or else he was going to levy charges and sanctions against the inmate and write him up in the form of an institutional charge.

When facing a monster that is determined to kill, steal, and destroy, they do not care about sanctions, charges, or something negative written about them. You will see leaders and nations around the world condemn demonstrative actions from someone or another nation, but that will have no effect as it relates to the monster, dictator, thug, abuser, tyrant, murderer, terrorists, or bullies' intentions.

Simply condemning someone's actions without taking action of your own is considered a weakness in the eyes of a monster, dictator, abuser, thug, or bully.

At some point, we must do more than just give our thoughts and prayers when we have the power to take action that could make a difference. Imagine seeing a homeless person sleeping on a park bench in freezing temperatures. We can give them our thoughts and prayers, or we can give them our thoughts, prayers, a sandwich, and one of our five coats that are sitting at the house that we never wear and are collecting dust in the backroom.

After seeing this weak display of inaction from leadership, the Monster appeared to become even more emboldened. The Monster has had more experience in finding and exploiting weaknesses in people than everyone in that hall combined. At that point, the team and I knew that we were going to fight for our fellow brothers. Three of my fellow officers were married with children, and one was getting married to his childhood sweetheart in a couple of weeks.

CHAPTER 4

FIGHT LIKE A CONQUEROR

As one lower-level supervisor, our breacher, who had worked tirelessly on the cell door with an arrangement of tools and equipment, discovered toilet paper and large amounts of hardened toothpaste that were jammed within the cell door. I observed the breacher pause for a moment; he then turned his head and looked back at us in fear. This supervisor, who was known for his strong work ethic, gave us a nod, and we knew that it was the moment that we had been waiting for. The supervisor began to count to three by signaling with his fingers and silently forming the words with his mouth.

As soon as he signaled one, not knowing that the Monster disabled the locking mechanism, the Monster rammed the cell door with his shoulders. Because we were on the wrong side of the door, we lost valuable seconds trying to engage the Monster. Sadly, the supervisor who was crouched down in front of the cell door working on the lock suffered serious injuries as the heavy steel door swung open with immense force, striking him on his head. The supervisor was knocked unconscious as blood began to stream down his head and face. A nurse on standby and in the area observed what transpired, and in a panic, she began to scream hysterically.

Bursting out of the cell appeared one of the largest figures we had ever seen. He was taller than the doorway and was wide as the doorway.

The Monster was completely naked and covered from head to toe in human waste. He roared like a lion and looked like a monster from a science fiction movie as he ripped off his homemade mask.

The Monster roared so loud and in such a manner that we could not hear nor communicate with one another to make any real-time adjustments. Each one of us was assigned to one body part: chest, right arm, left arm, right leg, and left leg. The Monster, who had been through more cell extractions than all of us combined, was armed with a large sharpened rusty piece of metal with a makeshift handle. Having the Monster running loose down the maximum-security hallway would be hard to stop. We needed to contain him in a smaller area like his cell.

The lead and prideful incident commander said nothing as he just stood there shaking while being paralyzed by fear. He was afraid to make a decision and chose to embrace fear when he needed to be courageous and take action. Other lower-ranked, quick-thinking, old-school supervisors sprang into action. One supervisor who had worked there for over twenty years had a shotgun filled with impact munitions and less-lethal ammo, and he started shooting the Monster. Someone threw some type of indoor flash grenade, and because of the acoustics in that tunnel of a hallway, our ears were ringing. Another seasoned supervisor began to shoot pepper ball rounds against the walls near the Monster and toward the Monster's upper torso area. I was covered in a reddish-orange oil-like substance as a couple of deployed MK-9 pepper spray canisters were utilized.

With the barrage of gunshot sounds, bangs, flashes of bright light, smoke, and loud yelling and screaming, it was like a scene from a movie. Thanks to the quick thinking of the lower-level supervisors who deployed the gas and other munitions, the Monster was distracted just enough, which bought us time to respond. Even though our tactical formation was broken because of being lined up on the wrong side of the door, we quickly regrouped.

As our tactical chain became tighter with no space in between the man in front of us, I had a decision to make. Instead of waiting for the onsite-incident commander to tell the team to engage the subject, I had to choose between either standing still and waiting for an incident commander who was frozen and controlled by fear to do nothing, or I—being the new guy—firmly tell the team to engage the Monster. I remembered the old saying, "I would rather ask for forgiveness than ask for permission," as I yelled, "MOVE! MOVE! MOVE!" while tapping the shoulder of the man in front of me. A train of close to 1,475 pounds began to move forward.

At that moment in the darkness, I could see the white sparks from the electric stun shield and hear that ever-so-familiar popping sound of 50,000 volts of electricity as our shield man with over 1,000 pounds of muscle behind him rammed the fully activated electric stun shield into the Monster's upper torso and midsection area.

Sometimes in life, we will encounter situations and circumstances that we know require us to take leadership and immediate action. We can hide behind the notion that we were waiting to receive an order, the right time, or sign to move as we pass the buck, procrastinate, overthink, adopt limiting beliefs, and shift the responsibility by casting blame; or we can choose to have a conqueror mindset and become courageous as we realize that inaction is influenced by fear. An army of pigeons led by an eagle is stronger that an army of eagles being led by a pigeon.

After the shield man slammed the fully activated stun shield into the monster's chest, we could see that the shield seemingly had no effect as it appeared to make the Monster even angrier. The Monster, knowing our tactics, knew that the prison leadership would bring the biggest and strongest officers to his cell. So, to counter that gesture, the Monster booby-trapped the floor in and around his cell area, making the floor very slippery. The combination of baby oil, lotion, urine, human waste, and sewage water made it very challenging just to stand up straight and maintain our balance without falling. It felt like we were standing on black ice.

In the cloud of smoke and flashing strobe lights, I could see that the Monster was towering over the shield man. It looked like a father looking down at his ten-year-old son.

As the 6'5", 350-pound shield man led the way as we pressed forward and tried to force the Monster backward, the Monster then grabbed the shield man, detaching him from our chain of officers as if he was a giant plucking a grape from a vine. After snatching the shield man off his feet, the Monster then pivoted like an oversized Olympic athlete performing a shotput, and with one thrust by using his momentum against him, he violently swung the shield man with immense force into his dark cell as if he just tossed a trash bag in a dumpster.

The shield man tried to regain his balance but instead slipped on the baby oil, lotion, water, and feces, almost as if he were a deer on ice, causing him to do a full split which we later found out tore his pants and his groin.

The shield man was in serious pain after sliding across the floor. His momentum falling forward was only stopped after he slammed his head against a reinforced concrete cell wall. This rendered the shield man unconscious.

At the time, seeing the biggest and heaviest man on our team folded up like a pretzel looked unreal. We all continued to be courageous as we fought hard and pressed forward. We were able to force the Monster deeper into his cell, or so we thought. It was almost as if the Monster was trying to create space between us and the group of supervisors who were armed with gas irritants and less-lethal weapons. Most violent cell extractions result in the offender trying to fight his way out of the cell.

The Monster seemed to know our game plan and our method of operation. It was as if we were playing checkers, and the Monster was playing chess. The Monster appeared to draw us in, almost as if we were pawns or small ants and he was a giant hairy spider luring us deeper into his web. During this highly volatile and stressful situation, I knew that smooth is fast and that I had to stay calm but aggressive. By having a conqueror mindset, I knew that instead of breathing high and tight, which would increase a person's chance to have anxiety and possibly go into panic, I needed to breathe low and slow. When faced with a stressful situation, the conqueror mindset teaches us that if we breathe low and slow from our diaphragm, it will help us slow things down and avoid tunnel vision when we are faced with a negative stimulus. In that moment, I knew that if the Monster got past us, he would take all the supervisors and staff members in the hallway hostage and try to torture us as he has done to victims in the past.

We were now in his domain and fighting for our lives. Even with the cell door open because of the poorly lit hallway, the Monster's cell was dark. It reminded me of being in a hot wet cave. It seemed as if the walls were sweating in the darkness, but because of the light from the hall, I could see human waste smeared all over the walls. Because of the slippery floor and walls, it was as if we were on a frozen lake covered in sewage. The stench was so bad that I had trouble breathing as my eyes, nose, and throat felt as if they were burning. The stench from the Monster's cell seemed to be worse than the chemical agents deployed. The combination of them both made it a struggle to see and breathe.

The Monster knew our tactics; he knew what angles we would take to restrain and subdue him. The Monster appeared to be one step ahead of us as he seemed to gain strength as he began to roar, grapple, elbow, kick, scratch, headbutt, bite, and swing several powerful punches at us. Because of my experience in hand-to-hand combat as I was fighting alongside my team, I took careful notice of the advanced dirty boxing, kickboxing, karate, Muay Thai, and Krav Maga striking combination moves that he was able to do nonstop and in sequence.

As large as the Monster was, he was incredibly strong, quick, and experienced and had extraordinary balance and endurance. This was a violent war of attrition, and I could see that my team members and I were in the room with something we had never encountered. This was an aggressive nonstop heavyweight fight between a titan and gladiators.

During the fight, the Monster tried to stab an officer, but his large shank became stuck between an officer's helmet and face shield. The officer froze for a brief moment, wondering if he was injured and if the knife penetrated his head; but in that time, the officer made a slight miscalculation, as he took a second too long to conduct a quick self-assessment in which he momentarily paused.

That brief moment of indecision and worry created an open window that gave the Monster an opportunity to exploit the weakness in the officer's body armor. In that split second when the officer paused, the Monster took advantage of that moment by punching him in the face with such force that it broke the officer's jaw. The officer hit the ground with his face completely disfigured and his mouth open, landing face-first on the cell floor in a pool of what appeared to be septic sewage.

After seeing this horrific site, a third officer seemed to have a panic attack as he started breathing high in his chest, taking short, quick breaths as he began trembling and shaking uncontrollably. Because of the erratic and inconsistent breathing patterns, the officer began hyperventilating and suddenly came down with a very bad case of hiccups. With the saturation of chemical agents deployed in the area, as well as the stomach-turning stench from the Monster's cell, the officer was having difficulty breathing, and he began to pound his chest with his fist.

Amid the chaos, after hearing the loud screaming from the officer—almost as if he could sense the fear—the Monster then focused his attention on the officer who was having a medical emergency. Almost as if it was in slow motion, like a large owl, the Monster awkwardly rotated his head and stared at the officer who was struggling to breathe and seemed to have difficulty processing what was about to happen next.

Seeing the officer who was once confident but now at his weakest point seemed to embolden the Monster who then focused on and targeted the officer once he felt that the roots of fear were planted deep enough in the mind of the officer that it would sow doubt big enough to make him second-guess himself, give up, and stop fighting.

I have found that in life, the enemy will always try his best to distract, discourage, and attack us when he thinks that we are at our weakest point. Like an enormous mosquito or leech, it seemed as if the Monster sucked out the officer's hope, peace, joy, purpose, confidence, and will to keep fighting.

Every battle starts in our minds. We must stay encouraged and inspired, rebuking the enemy in our lives. We must maintain a conqueror mindset when we are in a battle and throughout the day. Only then can we walk in love and seize the day.

We were fighting the Monster, and it was almost as if we were in the middle of a hurricane or a tornado. I knew that we could not just weather the storm; we had to conquer it.

As the fight prolonged and intensified, we were all fighting through pain and sustaining injuries. The situation in the cell was not good; we needed immediate backup. The Monster, while fighting all of us, appeared to be focusing on us one at a time, like a great white shark smelling blood in the water while attacking a school of fish. The Monster used his body weight and rammed the screaming officer seemly, crushing him into the steel bunk bed area in the cell. Because of the hard impact and the odd angle where the officer was hit; he suffered a serious back injury.

The officer's back was injured so badly that he made a loud bloodcurdling scream for help toward the group of supervisors who were in the hallway right outside the door. Even with all the loud screaming, banging sounds, calling for help, and roaring sounds coming out of the cell, the group of supervisors stood in the hallway frozen in fear as they chose not to assist or step foot in the cell.

When people talk about human stress responses, they talk about the fight-or-flight response, but what they forget to mention is the freeze response.

Instead of coming into the dark cell to join the fight and help the seriously injured officers, the supervisors chose to freeze.

Understanding that people could have made a difference in that situation but chose not to because of fear reminded me of an animal show where dozens of zebras or buffalo were grazing in a large circle, protecting one another. The group had the numbers and appeared to look formidable until that full-grown lion rushed in. As the lion attacked, the zebras and buffalo all fell back and watched in agony from a safe distance; some of them turned and looked the other way, and others began grazing, acting like they did not hear or see what was going on right in front of them.

We may hear some people talk about their circle or the people in their circle. In life, it is not about who's in your circle: it's about who's in your corner. That person in your corner needs to be you. This is why we need to stop speaking negativity in our lives. We must stop the negative self-talk. No one should love you more than you love yourself. Who really has your back if the worst-case scenario occurred to you? You will always find out who people really are in an emergency.

With three warriors seriously injured and in need of immediate medical attention, the number 4 officer and I were meeting force with force as we no longer followed the approved unsuccessful restraining techniques that we were taught. We realized that we were in a life-and-death fight for survival, and we could not rely on outdated methods that we knew, in real time, were not working.

At that time, I remembered the old saying, "Would you rather be judged by twelve or carried by six?" In response to the Monster trying to headbutt, stab, eye gouge, and bite us, we continued to swing several punches and kicks in defense. While giving the Monster verbal commands to stop resisting, I could see that the Monster had no respect for the rule of law; he had a simple objective. His objective was to kill and destroy.

The Monster swung a punch that was so powerful to the body of the officer next to me that the 6'4", approximately 300-pound officer slammed against the wall and dropped to his knees as he curled up in a fetal position, gasping for air. Little did I know that his ribs were broken.

While fighting the Monster, I observed the officer lying in the sewage water on the floor gasping for air. Not only was I the smallest person in the room, but in that moment, I also realized that I was the only officer left fighting. When having a conqueror mindset, we have to come to the understanding that sometimes in life, there will be no backup on the way. Sometimes you have to be your own hero and save yourself from whatever monster you may be facing.

In that moment, I knew that I could not waste my energy being upset with the circumstance or angry with the people who I expected, or thought would help me. I had to redirect my focus to the Monster in front of me that presented a clear and present danger. By utilizing the conqueror mindset, I knew that action was the direct opposition to fear.

In the moment, I knew that I had to win to save the lives of my coworkers so that they did not succumb to their injuries, go into shock, cardiac arrest, or drown in the septic and now blood-filled sewage water.

As I continued striking the Monster with punches and kicks, I could sense that my strikes were barely slowing down his attacks. I will never forget punching the Monster in the body as hard as I could only to feel as if my strikes were being absorbed by fat and muscle. I have never punched an elephant seal before, but that is the body structure that the Monster had.

I then reached up and punched the Monster several times in the face just to find myself being slammed against a slippery wall as the Monster extended both of his arms and grabbed my neck in a front choke technique. The Monster's arms were so long that I could barely reach him. His arms were slippery and covered in fecal matter and baby oil.

I remember hearing loud hysterical screaming from the prison nurse in the hall outside of the cell, as well as the loud yelling and arguing between supervisors in the hall. In addition to the yelling and panic calls for assistance coming from an injured officer who was still conscious in the cell, the Monster seemed to be getting stronger in the chaos, panic, and confusion as he roared even louder.

As the Monster's grip on my throat intensified, I could see that this Monster was trying to kill me. As the pressure from the Monster's choke seemed to be tighter than a vise grip and stronger than the jaws of life, in my mind, I thought there was no way out. At that moment, I realized that the armor that I had on had no effect. I knew that I had to have a conqueror mindset in order to not only survive this attack but also conquer this enemy. I had to clear my mind, be in the moment, challenge any limiting beliefs and negative thoughts, breathe low and slow, and tell my mind what to think.

Having a conqueror mindset allows us to become a prudent and a wise person and to have the ability to slow things down, block out and eliminate distractions, see the desired outcome, make a blueprint and a battle plan in real time, and take appropriate action all within a fraction of a second. Having a conqueror mindset allows people to be equipped with the three most advanced and effective weapon systems in the universe namely knowledge, wisdom, and understanding. If applied properly, a person will learn to stop fighting to win: They will learn how to fight like a conqueror and know that they have already won. A conqueror wins in war, one that overcomes adversity, subjugates, subdues, vanquishes, defeats others, and is a winner.

If we go through life trying to fight to win, we may find ourselves being tense and telegraphing our punches and growing tired and weary. But if we fight like a conqueror knowing that we have already won, we will find ourselves fighting smoothly and with confidence, which will allow us to be able to stay calm when faced with a storm. When faced with opposition or adversity, the fighter or warrior will simply try to do their best to win while the conqueror will know that they have already won. Just like a fight, we can choose to walk through life tight and full of stress, or we can choose to have a conqueror mentality and mindset and walk through life loose and smooth while reaching and conquering every objective and fear.

I had previously been in several life-and-death situations in my life where I had to fight against insurmountable odds. This situation was different. I was fighting against an enemy that appeared to be gaining strength and had every advantage. I knew that I had to be transformed and that the transformation had to begin with the renewing of my mind.

Once I implemented the conqueror mindset strategy in that moment, I immediately began to increase my faith and believe that I was not only going to survive this deadly encounter, but I was also going to win and conquer this enemy.

I had to tell my mind to tell my body not to give up and to win. We have the power to tell our mind to tell our body what to do. If we ever had to tell ourselves to get up and do something, or if we had ever said the words *Let's go* or *You can do it*, that is us utilizing the conqueror mindset system and not knowing it. Our mind is like our lungs, heart, fingers, and so forth. Our mind belongs to us. So, the next time a negative thought tries to enter our mind, we need to remember that we have the power and authority in us to challenge and conquer any negative thought of doubt, negative self-talk, self-sabotage, worry, anxiety, stress, or fear.

I understood that the Monster's objective in life was to kill, steal, and destroy. For him to do that, he needed to make me believe that he was in control and that his grip was suffocating me. I could see that for the Monster to win, he had a strategy that he knew worked for him. His strategy was to intimidate, distract, and overwhelm people; and once the person lost their focus, they would become anxious and discouraged. This is when the Monster would come from the darkness, attack, gain control, and overwhelm them.

Having a conqueror mindset allowed me to slow things down and immediately think of other forces on earth that have the same fighting tactics and techniques. I was able to think back to my childhood when I first created the conqueror mindset. I remember how I was always standing up and fighting against older bullies—no matter what size or how many there were. If the bullies were trying to harm and take advantage of others, I would step in the gap no matter the circumstance. After coming home each day from school, I would exercise and study martial arts. In addition, I had a unique hobby where I would study insects' and animals' mindsets, attitudes, behaviors, fighting styles, tactics, techniques, and abilities. I admired the mindset of the lion—which I felt was the king of land—and the eagle, which was the king of the air.

By implementing a conqueror mindset, I recognized the fighting style of the Monster, which then gave me knowledge, wisdom, and understanding. I realized that some of the Monster's tactics were similar to a crocodile. Crocodiles are very aggressive and dangerous predators; they are mostly nocturnal animals. They spend most of their time hiding in the darkest shadows in shallow water, but they are also known for coming out of the water and on land where they hide in plain sight. When in the water, crocodiles are very powerful, quick, and comfortable.

When they emerge, in many cases, they shock, intimidate, and frighten their prey, causing them to panic and become overwhelmed with stress and anxiety. This style of attack causes animals to freeze or try to run as they drag their prey or victim back into the deep dark depths from which it came. I noticed that like a crocodile, the Monster used his cell like a habitat; and in the slippery oil and septic water, he was fast and hard to manage.

Just like a spider, this Monster liked to hide in dark clutter-filled areas as he loved to ambush his victims and prey. Like a negative thought, phobia, childhood trauma, addiction, stress, anxiety, or fear, if our mind is filled with clutter, it provides the negative stimuli more places to hide. By getting rid of the clutter, the invader will have no place to hide, making him easier to spot.

Like a mouse or a roach, they would prefer a clutter-filled house to invade rather than a clean, neat, and organized home any day of the week simply because it does not want to be exposed.

By acquiring a conqueror mindset, we will have the ability to clear the clutter and win.

Just like a spider on the hunt, many of them like to stay along corners and walls, utilizing angles and leverage to their strength. With the Monster knowing that it weighed beyond 400 pounds, he used the walls and the bolted-down metal bunk bed for balance. It was like I was fighting a large snapping turtle in a dark wet muddy hole.

At that moment, I developed a sense of clarity. I understood what the Monster's real name was. It was fear. Using the conqueror mindset, I understood that an unpleasant emotion caused by the belief that something or someone is dangerous or likely to cause pain or a threat to oneself—whether that potential pain is real or imagined—is, by definition, called *fear*.

It can not only seem to be very challenging to combat fear, but it can also be rewarding because of the opportunity that it presents for us to be courageous and find self, peace, joy, and freedom in that process. Fear, in many cases, is accompanied by stress and anxiety. Training could only prepare me for so much; I had to become very calm and go back to the last time I felt unpleasant and remember that I had victory.

Once I did that, I began to think of a positive outcome of me defeating this Monster. I had to manifest greatness by having a conqueror mindset, which gave me a better sense of awareness. The story of David and Goliath immediately came to my mind. David had to fight against a lion and a bear to prepare him for Goliath. Sometimes in life, we must go through the struggle, hurt, pain, and the process to prepare us for the battle that is going to transform us into the person that we are supposed to be.

More so than just the training and past work experiences where I had to fight, arrest, and detain serial killers, terrorists, cannibals, child predators, rapists, bank robbers, prison escapees, and more, I remember fighting older bullies in school since I was in kindergarten. I knew that everything that I had been through my entire life prepared me for this one moment in time.

By having renewed faith and letting go of limiting beliefs, I was able to slow things down in my mind with a sense of clarity because I now had a new focus. With that focus, I was able to shut out all the overwhelming stimuli that were previously distracting me. I knew that in my current mindset, I would not be successful, so I had to utilize the conqueror mindset that I invented to transform. For me to transform, it had to start with the renewing of my mind. When I did that, almost like trying to thread a needle or shoot a target from a long range, I became laser focused. Suddenly, the overstimulation of the senses stopped. All the loud screaming, the horrible stench, and the sight of blood and injured coworkers only made me more focused on the task at hand, which was conquering the Monster.

Once I realized that I had the power and capacity to control my mind, only then was my mind able to control my body. After I commanded my mind to calm down, and by accepting the fact that I was not in control of the situation, I developed a sense of peace and inner strength. I knew that I could not win on my own strength and that I could not lean on my own understanding. I had to tell myself that I was in control of my mind, body, and my response to the stimuli.

After speaking to myself and praying, I asked my Creator, who is the source of my strength, for the knowledge, wisdom, and understanding to win. After fully realizing that I was not in control of the situation, it allowed me the ability to be in control of myself.

I have found that some people want to be in control, and because of this, they either try too hard or they develop a type of attitude, behavior, and mindset that are not conducive to success. We all want to have a great day, for our loved ones to overcome a health challenge, or for the weather to be perfect for our outdoor activity. We have to understand that in life, sometimes things do not work out the way we had planned, expected, or hoped.

Once we obtain a conqueror mindset, we will learn to relinquish that power if things do not work out the way we had planned, or if our expectation is not met. We must realize that we can only control what we can control. As long as we do the best that we can, we will always win. Doing this reduces and eliminates the fear of failure, which then opens a door for us to overcome and conquer the monster in front of us.

After humbling myself to this notion, I then achieved a state of mindfulness. I suddenly felt a sense of peace and strength almost as if I was in the eye of a storm. I was able to stay calm in the middle of chaos. In that moment, I realized who I really was. I was not a title or position anymore: I was more than a conqueror.

If the sink or the tub in our lives is overflowing, instead of us scrambling for towels and blankets to soak up the water, we need to have a conqueror mindset, which will enable us to slow down and realize that all we have to do is turn off the faucet.

As I was able to conduct the conqueror mindset's breathing method of breathing low and slow, I was able to gain confidence, and it seemed as if everything was more manageable and moving in slow motion. When you are fighting for your life, you can choose to give up, or you can choose to fight like a conqueror and win. By utilizing the conqueror mindset, almost as if within a tenth of a second, I was able to better process everything around me as I glanced and suddenly noticed, while quickly scanning the dark room, that the Monster broke all the light fixtures and that he covered all the windows, preventing any light from entering in his cell. I could see that this Monster preferred dwelling in the darkness. I quickly had a better understanding of the mind of the Monster.

I understood that the Monster felt anchored, his strongest and most comfortable, in the darkness. I knew that to take away his strength, I had to make him uncomfortable and had to expose him to the light. I began to think of all the things that I overcame in my life, and instead of feeling unpleasant or uncomfortable, I became empowered.

In this almost surreal moment in time, I realized that I was in fact in the room with the Monster and that the Monster affected every person differently.

CHAPTER 5

WE ARE MORE THAN CONQUERORS

I realized that in my own strength and understanding, there was no kick or punch that I could deliver strong enough to hurt the Monster in a significant manner. Even though in martial arts training I had broken boards and bricks with my fist and elbows, I could not generate enough force to slow down or stop the Monster.

At this point, I was fighting for more than just myself. My mind quickly reminded me that my four other team members who were larger than me fought the Monster and were overpowered. In a split second, a negative thought slipped into my mind, asking me, *How long do you think you can hold on? You can't last. You can't win.* I immediately recognized those negative thoughts, and by utilizing the conqueror mindset system, I immediately challenge those negative thoughts with positive thoughts and affirmations.

Having a conqueror mindset encouraged me to tell myself that the fight was not over until I won.

When faced with anxiety, PTSD, phobias, adversity, stress, addiction, trauma, and fear, we have to remember to identify and challenge any negative self-talk or limiting beliefs that may try to pop up in our minds. This monster or negative stimuli, in some cases, will reveal itself in the form of an emotional trigger. With a conqueror mindset, we will recognize the source, origin, and root cause of our fear, which will enable us to eliminate, uproot, and conquer self-sabotage, self-doubt, and other self-destructive and self-injurious behaviors that are designed to distract and discourage us from winning our battle and having peace.

With a conqueror mindset, we will learn that we have the power to let go of the fear of the unknown. If we do the absolute best in all that we do, we will never lose. Having a conqueror mindset allowed me to have faith and believe what I was taught growing up: The fight does not go to the swift nor the strong but to those who can endure until the end.

I was not only going to survive, but I was also going to win. I told myself that the only way I was going to leave that cell was when I won. I utilized the conqueror mindset as I targeted the weakest area on the Monster. I targeted the Monster's appendages in a very intentional and concise manner. I grabbed the Monster's right fingers and thumb.

As soon as I altered and manipulated his appendages in such a manner that made the Monster feel uncomfortable, the Monster looked at me in the eyes for the first time. He looked at me in shock as we shared a brief moment where he and I both knew that he was no longer in control. This was one of those eye-opening, life-changing moments for both of us.

After being placed in a pain compliance finger-and-wrist lock, the Monster made a sharp yell and then suddenly became quiet. I will never forget hearing complete silence as the Monster started tapping his chest with his left hand as if he was giving me a tap out or a universal sign of surrender.

Once I transformed myself with the renewing of my mind, I felt as if I could move mountains. Now in real time, as I looked at the Monster in front of me, I had no fear. Having no fear allowed me to now have the ability to move and control this Monster. Like a bit in a horse's mouth or like a rudder at the end of a ship, it only took a couple of pounds of pressure to guide this large monster in any direction that I wanted. After being truthful with myself about how I felt in that moment, I felt a type of inner peace. In that state of mind, I began to recognize that anxiety and excitement were both states of high activation of emotions. Excitement was attached to joy as anxiety was influenced by fear. I recognized that I had the power to choose. I chose excitement, which gave me what felt like superpowers and allowed me to have no fear of the Monster. I discovered that fear can be crippling while the excitement and living with expectancy can renew our strength. My mind, body, and spirit felt renewed. By simply changing my state of mind and taking action, I felt transformed. I first was truthful with myself and how I truly felt in that moment.

If we learn to be completely honest with ourselves and how we truly feel in every situation, we will find ourselves with a better sense of awareness and clarity. Having a conqueror mindset will enable us to achieve one of the highest states of mindfulness, which enables us to attain knowledge, wisdom, and understanding of self as well as any stimuli around us. It's time for us to stop overthinking and to simplify our lives. By doing this, I began to have a different perception and perspective of myself in relation to my circumstance.

By having a conqueror mindset, it changed the position and the angle from which I viewed myself. Once I gained knowledge, wisdom, and understanding of myself, I realized that I was no longer going to allow myself to think that I was the victim or the underdog. I realized that I was more than a conqueror. The Monster was like a large hairy spider, and instead of me allowing him to make me feel as if I was an ant caught in his web, I adopted a conqueror mindset. In that moment when I changed the way I viewed myself, it changed the way I viewed my circumstance.

I realized that I was the boot, and I had the power to conquer the Monster by smashing my own limiting beliefs and eliminating any negative self-talk that was holding me back from being victorious. I was in the same physical location with the same stimuli in front of me, but utilizing the conqueror mindset changed the way I thought about myself in relation to my circumstance which then altered my outcome. We have to remember that our destiny and outcome in life are influenced by our actions, and our actions are influenced by our state of mind.

Having a conqueror mindset will enable us to achieve a state of mindfulness, which will assist us in obtaining knowledge, wisdom, and understanding of self, as well as any stimuli around us.

It's time for us to stop overthinking, and to simplify our lives. While creating our own path in the forest of life, we need to stop using a dull ax and later wonder why we are full of blisters. By utilizing a conqueror mindset, we will have the knowledge, skills, and ability to first sharpen our ax, which will allow us to get more done with less energy and in less time.

I remember seeing the Monster whining in pain as he appeared to be smiling at me, showing his large yellowish and gray teeth that he filed down to sharp points. Through gridded teeth and almost in a growl, he said that he would be good if I let him go. I knew not to trust, negotiate with, come to a common ground, or learn to cope with the Monster. I have learned that just because someone is smiling at you does not mean that they have friendly intentions; on the contrary, they may in fact be a wolf growling at you showing you his teeth, or a snake with a forked tongue waiting for an opportunity to strike.

Knowing this, instead of letting go of him, I tightened up my grip. I understood that words are powerful and that life and death are in the power of the tongue. Because of this notion, after speaking life and declaring victory in my situation, I decided to speak to the Monster. I set the expectation, and I boldly told the Monster that I was in control.

We may hear some people tell us that we should think of fear as a passenger in life that we need to cope with. By having a conqueror mindset, we will learn that it is healthy for us to respect but challenge that ideology.

Say, for example, you arrive back home and you discover that a strange person you do not know has unlawfully entered your home and is now lying in your bed. Are you going to cope with this squatter or invader and accept them as a passenger on your journey in life? Are you going to keep quiet, be too afraid to rock the boat, afraid of making some waves because you want to keep the peace, stay under the radar, keep your head down, and nervously crawl into bed begging and hoping that this stranger will not violate you in the middle of the night? Or are we going to be honest with the way we feel and be bold enough to know our value, say no, draw a line in the sand as we establish a standard with healthy boundaries, and command this monster to leave as we drag them out of our house and out of our life, kicking and screaming?

Just like a negative thought that enters our mind, we have the power and authority to choose to take action and identify, confront, and conquer that negative thought so that we can live in peace and with freedom.

Fear is not here to tuck us in at night; fear is here to violate, kill, steal, and destroy us. The people who tell us that we must learn to cope and live with fear are the same people who are secretly struggling with fear.

We will hear many people tell us how to approach and handle fear. Some may tell us that we should live with it and accept fear as a part of our daily life. By having a conqueror mindset, we will now understand and know that we cannot suppress, ignore, turn our back on, or run away from fear.

We have to be courageous as we gain knowledge, wisdom, and understanding of that fear and conquer it. For example, if someone asks you to conduct a presentation to a group of young children in reference to the life of an eagle a month from now, you may initially feel uncomfortable; but if you were to study and gain knowledge, wisdom, and understanding in reference to eagles, you would feel qualified and more confident to speak about all matters concerning that particular topic.

Because you put in the work to gain this knowledge, you will have no fear when conducting your presentation. Knowledge is power but only to the people who take action based on that knowledge. A conqueror understands that our preparation, discipline, attitude, and mindset are interconnected. This is the conqueror mindset blueprint on how to handle fear. Many of us may have seen the hundreds of videos of small children and adults at the zoo looking at the big cats or wolves. It was exciting looking at the large predator through the thick glass, but as soon as the child or adult turned their back to the predator, the predator instinctively attacked the glass behind them.

This is how the monster of fear works. Like a wolf, the monster wants us to panic so that he can chase us down when we turn our backs to run; or like a fox, he may appear to be playful, but unbeknownst to us, he was actually stalking us and luring us closer to his fox hole. The wolf and the fox have two different methods of attack, but they have the same goal. Just like the Monster, they are highly intelligent; they know the forest and woods better than any other animal; and their goal is to kill, steal, and destroy.

With that being said, we have to stop settling for crumbs and accepting this passive approach of coping or acting like we do not see the proverbial elephant in the room in reference to fear.

The next time someone tells us to live through it and cope with something that we know in our heart is unacceptable, we must consider the source. Some of these people may have good intentions, and some do not. If they were honest, some of them are all bark and no bite because, in truth, they have never faced real adversity. They have never been in a fight, but they are quick to tell you to throw the first punch.

They preach to us about discipline and good habits, but they do the complete opposite. Let's not be distracted or discouraged by hypocritical people who consistently disqualify themselves. Let's stay focused and run like a race horse with blinders on, staying focused, present, in the moment, and excited about the future. As we live within our purpose and pursue what has been planted in us, let's not look to the left or the right. Let's stay inspired and not get distracted. Let's not share our big dreams and visions with small-minded people. Let's walk by faith and not by sight as we stay focused, on the narrow path, and on our journey in life.

As people, we are blessed to be the most powerful creatures on the planet. This is because of the power of our mindset and our imagination. We cannot allow people who have a pessimistic view of the world and themselves hinder us from walking in our purpose. Once we do this, we will be able to identify the enemy and have the courage to command victory in our lives and tell the monster of fear that they are not in charge.

I spoke directly to the Monster and gave him a clear signal in plain words as I let him know that he was not in charge. There was no doubt that this Monster was my enemy. I did not hate the Monster, but I hated what he represented: his actions, behavior, mood, attitude, disposition, and mindset. By not hating the Monster, I did not become a Monster myself. By walking in love instead of hate, I was able to walk with ease as the Monster walked through life struggling and with difficulty.

Walking in love is not a passive action. Walking in love is a strength and means that we are living life intentionally, in truth, and with healthy boundaries. When we have healthy boundaries, we will be honest with ourselves and the way that we feel which will allow us to have peace and know what we will and will not tolerate in our lives.

After speaking to the Monster, I then took action. I began to walk out of the dark cell, still holding onto the Monster's right arm, wrist, and finger in a controlled hold. By utilizing the conqueror mindset, I have discovered that once we clearly identify what the monster is in our lives, in many cases, we have to be courageous and go back to that dark place and drag that monster out of the darkness and into the light so that we can have clarity and free ourselves from the monster's stranglehold in our lives.

As the Monster and I exited the cell, one of the injured officers who was in the cell sitting in the septic water said, along with a group of curse words and profane speech, "Great job!" as he referred toward the Monster finally being subdued and controlled.

Once I came out of the darkness and into the poorly lit hallway, I heard silence as several supervisors and staff members just looked on in shock. I then set the expectation as I told the Monster that we were going to walk down the hall and to an adjacent unit where I was going to place him in a suicide prevention cell. I told the Monster that if he did not obey my direct order, then I would increase the tension on my control hold to gain voluntary compliance.

As the Monster and I continued to walk down the hallway, every inmate in that unit stood almost as if they were at attention and in complete silence and looked out their small windows at us as if they were in shock. Supervisors and staff members, while holding their noses because of the smell of the Monster, appeared to be nervous and surprised as I was able to escort the Monster down the hall with our arms interlocked.

As we entered another secure area that had a reinforced suicide cell, with the assistance of staff members holding the door, I was able to place this now-humbled, defeated, subdued, broken, and conquered Monster in a different cell without further incident.

I ordered him to put on a green suicide prevention smock that was in the cell, and without delay, he complied with my direct order.

Later, I was informed that up until his transfer, the Monster remained subdued and never gave any other staff member a problem.

Sometimes in life, we may feel something that we can't fully explain—a monster is trying to get a hold of us, choke us, and suffocate us. Whatever the fear, worry, phobia, stress, or negative stimuli we are facing, we must realize that we can utilize the conqueror mindset and fight like a conqueror.

This monster comes in different forms: stress, fear, childhood trauma, anxiety, depression, negative self-talk, anger, overthinking, jealousy, unforgiveness, hatred, bigotry, slothfulness, gluttony, lust, pride, selfishness, arrogance, self-sabotage, phobias, insecurity, procrastination, panic, racism, hatred, abandonment, post-traumatic stress, overthinking, worry, self-doubt, and the like.

By implementing the conqueror mindset, we will be able to identify the sources of these feelings and thoughts at the root as we will now have the ability to stay calm which will then give us the opportunity to develop a strategy, blueprint, and battle plan to uproot, extract, and conquer the monster.

In many circumstances, the Monster will do his very best to distract and discourage us in order to weaken our defenses just enough to allow him the opportunity to slip in. The Monster, if undetected and unchallenged, will then try to hide deep in our subconscious mind; and from the shadows, he will rear his ugly head to try to overwhelm and destroy us.

As we fight like a conqueror when using the conqueror mindset, we will quickly recognize that the monster is the enemy and wants to steal our joy and our peace. He wants to kill our hopes, dreams, relationships, our physical body, our careers, and future. The Monster will always lie to us. He will threaten us with major attacks while attacking us.

He will attempt to work an angle as he will try to entice us with money, promotion, possessions, fame, or a good time. The Monster is a con man who is trying to sell us the idea that he is in charge. The Monster is looking for weakness within us because behind the smoke screen and mirrors is a desperate and insecure predator who knows that he is already defeated.

The Monster has a sensitive and fragile ego. When we fight back, the Monster will always find a way to play the victim. He wants to camouflage himself like a chameleon and embed himself like a tick in our minds while attempting to suck the life out of us. Like an abusive partner, the Monster is miserable and takes joy in tearing us down, hoping to make us feel like it is our fault and trying to discourage us. Like being bitten by a Komodo dragon holding us captive, the Monster wants to numb and paralyze us with complacency and fear as he tries to poison our minds.

The Monster along with its many forms is a master at mind games and manipulation. He wants us to develop a type of Stockholm syndrome as we began to bond, cope, and try to gain feelings of affection for the monster of addiction, eating disorders, depression, limiting beliefs, and fear. By having a conqueror mindset, we will recognize the schemes and tricks of the enemy, which will allow us to resist him. As we resist the enemy he will flee.

His goal is to destroy everything that we worked for—love—and hold dear.

If we fight to win, we may sometimes feel overwhelmed and anxious and grow tired; but if we fight as if we have already won, it will confuse the enemy, thus allowing us to have a tactical advantage. We will be loose, free-flowing, and spontaneous while the enemy will be tight, desperate, and predictable.

From this day forward, it is time for us to realize that we are stronger than the enemy of addiction, stress, phobias, anxiety, childhood trauma, worry, and fear. We will no longer be a survivor, fighter, or warrior simply fighting to win, which in time will make us feel fatigued. Instead, we will now become a conqueror, which will allow us to operate on a higher frequency. By utilizing the conqueror mindset, we will have a conqueror mentality and mindset, understanding that we are a conqueror and we have conquered the Monster.

CHAPTER 6

KNOWLEDGE, WISDOM, AND UNDERSTANDING

For the people present that day, the Monster changed our lives forever. For others, the Monster may be an analogy. In life, every person on the planet will be confronted with a monster. The monster's fighting style, appearance, and method of attack are different for every person. Some people may feel it in the pit of their stomach almost as if the monster is stalking them in their subconscious mind. For others, this monster may be in the forefront of their minds, affecting them daily and at a conscious level. While this monster may only emerge from the shadows when there is an emotional trigger, for other people, it may resemble stress, depression, fear, PTSD, anxiety, jealousy, hatred, addiction, childhood trauma, greed, negative self-talk, anger, phobias, procrastination, worry, self-doubt, pride, unforgiveness, disorders, and the like.

This monster is the same monster, but it will appear to each of us differently with the same goal. By finally saying enough is enough, it is up to us to have a conqueror mindset and recognize that we are no longer going to allow this negative stimulus to control our lives.

As we are conquering the monster in our lives, no matter what form the monster is in, we must realize that right now, we are the youngest that we will ever be, and we are the oldest that we have ever been. Think about that for a moment. We cannot get any younger than we are in this present moment in time. With that being said, this is the perfect time in the present for us to make a positive lasting change for our future. The best time to get rid of and conquer those unhealthy habits, attitudes, behaviors, and mindset is right now. Let's not wait until we have no sand left in our hourglass to make a change.

Some people, who may have acronyms behind their name or have a large influence, may tell us that all we need to do to overcome fear, stress, and anxiety is to think happy thoughts. If there is a man standing in front of you who is armed stating that he is going to kill you, thinking happy thoughts is not going to save you.

Happy thoughts alone are not going to help us when we are under attack by a relentless monster. We need to take action. The monster is not going to pause and take a time out with you so that you can catch your breath and get yourself together.

Like most predators, the monster prefers their prey to either run, hide, give up, or ignore them. He wants to chase them down from behind or attack them from a blind spot. The monster is hoping that we will be on the fence, indecisive, cope with them, play coy, and be lukewarm as we shy away from the fight, tight roping our way through life. Having a conqueror mindset encourages us to immediately recognize and change the dying batteries in the smoke alarm of our life. Instead of sitting back and ignoring the loud piercing alarms and beeping sounds that go off in our lives acting as if everything is okay, we will have the courage to get out of our comfort zone and change the battery. If we are watching something we don't like on television, we need to have a conqueror mindset and change the channel, which will allow us to break away from poor programming and operate at a higher frequency.

The Monster wants us to blindly defer and bend to his will. The Monster is like a wolf; he is looking for a sheep to slaughter and devour. As a conqueror, we will surprise that conniving wolf when he realizes that he walked into a cage with a lion. We need to stop tap-dancing around issues, habits, addictions, fears, and mindsets that are not aligned with our vision for peace, joy, freedom, happiness, and purpose.

We must stop allowing ourselves to fall asleep at the wheel, only later to find ourselves in a ditch.

With a conqueror mindset, we will understand that when it comes to our mental health and overall wellness, we have to be our own advocates. Let's stop waiting for someone else to save us. It is time for us to be our own superheroes by having a conqueror mindset. We are going to stop walking on eggshells, not knowing our value while continuing to compare ourselves to others and allowing other people to plant that negative seed of doubt, jealousy, anxiety, and fear in our minds.

By having a conqueror mindset, we will be courageous enough to do what is right even if it is not popular. We will understand the power of saying no as we now will have the ability to create healthy boundaries in our lives. These boundaries are established in love. Whether with family, friends, or associates, by utilizing the conqueror mindset, we now will have the ability to love people from a distance.

Sometimes in life, the person who may seem to bother you the most may be a friend or even a family member. By having a conqueror mindset, we will learn to choose peace over drama and distance over disrespect. We will learn to have patience, forgiveness, and love for others; but in order to do that, we need to first have patience, forgiveness, and love for ourselves.

Quite a few people say that they are looking for love and someone to complete them; it is impossible to find love or give real love to someone else if we are not walking in it ourselves. Self-doubt is influenced by not understanding our self-worth. This is influenced by people not having self-love. As we better understand what it means to have a conqueror mindset, we will find that we have a choice to make. We can walk in fear, or we can choose to walk in love. By having a conqueror mindset, we will be filled with so much love that it will leave no room for hate. We will have an overflow of love that will then change the way we walk, talk, and think. Only with that overflow can we be ready to express that love to someone else wholeheartedly. A conqueror knows that in battle, if we have hatred in our hearts, we have already lost. Hate leads to defeat, and love conquers all.

With a conqueror mindset, we will understand that we must be our biggest advocates as we relate to our mental health, safety, and overall wellness.

Some people continue to passively address the weeds in the garden, but with a conqueror mindset, we will have the courage to dig in and pull the weeds out by the root and cast it in the fire. We must stop being passive when it comes to our overall wellness. We must live life intentionally.

Fighting the monster is like battling a fire; some people get distracted by the smoke and large flames. Instead of focusing on the flames and allowing ourselves to suffocate in the smoke, we need to simply focus on the source or the base of that fire. For many of us, the source of that fire—fear, insecurity, worry, stress, disorder, panic, phobia, anxiety, childhood trauma, and monster—comes from our past experiences, specific situations, and the stories and fears that were passed down from others.

We cannot standby, dismiss, or ignore the volcano in our life that is building pressure.

We must be courageous and address the pressure, stress, trauma, and monster, or else, in time, we will suffer the consequences. When conquering the monster in our lives, we have to open up our eyes and realize that unfortunately, many of us were subjected to certain types of trauma growing up. Some of us were introduced and exposed to childhood stories, songs, and nursery rhymes that planted fear in the hearts and minds of us as little children. In these stories, children were harmed, eaten by wolves, cooked by old ladies with large stoves, drowned by men playing music on a flute, and so forth. Unknowing parents and teachers were downloading and installing the negative program of fear on to the hard drive of our minds. Planting this monster of fear in the minds of a child at such a young age was like allowing a deadly snake to wait under a rock.

Like planting a weed in the fertile soil of a child's mind, some weeds have the ability to mimic and camouflage with their surroundings. Every person's situation is different. For many of us, this monster of trauma was much more than just a story; it was a clear and present real danger.

A conqueror mindset allows us the opportunity to rediscover ourselves at the core and to break free from negative programming. We all have experienced circumstances and situations that have affected us in different ways. We cannot allow that situation to define us, set us back, or hinder us from our true purpose. By having a conqueror mindset, we will be able to reclaim control. We have to first stop running from this monster of fear and trauma. Once we recognize and acknowledge that it did happen, we will learn to forgive ourselves which will allow us to forgive others. We will unlearn bad behaviors, attitudes, and biases. With a conqueror mindset, we will understand the power of unlearning negative programming. This will now give us the ability to break down the origins of any negative perceptions, perspectives, behaviors, attitudes, biases, anxieties, or fears that may exist. By doing this, we will find out who we really are and who it is that we want to be.

By utilizing the conqueror mindset, we will be able to identify our triggers; find the origin of that feeling toward those triggers and challenges; and eliminate those negative ideologies and replace them with a positive belief system.

A conqueror mindset teaches us that we have the power to be patient, take a moment for ourselves, and evaluate how we truly feel in any given circumstance.

You may hear some people say the term moving forward as it relates to a person who has gone through a particular experience. They are mistaken; there is no such thing as moving forward until you conquer the monster or negative stimuli. If you simply move forward, you are ignoring the stimulus or monster; and in time, it will get stronger and chase you down from behind. By having a conqueror mindset, we will have an attitude of gratitude. We will have no fear of sudden disasters, and we will learn to walk in love and with expectancy.

By attaining a conqueror mindset, we will understand that when we operate in truth, it allows us to be rooted within a solid foundation. Once we establish a strong foundation, we will keep our feet on solid ground not giving the enemy a foothold in our life.

By doing this, we will be able to withstand all the seasons and the upcoming storms ahead.

A conqueror understands that fear, stress, anxiety, addiction, and the like are monsters. If ignored or pacified, the monster has the ability to become so large that it will affect us in every aspect of our lives. It can start off as a thought, situation from our childhood, bad habit, or fear; and over time through stress and trauma, it could affect our physical and mental health and wellness. If left unchallenged, like a weed, it will grow roots and expand, trying to take over the garden of our mind.

CHAPTER 7

CONQUER OUR OUTCOMES

Some people say that time heals all wounds. In my experience, I have found that statement to be incorrect. With certain wounds, if not addressed and attended to immediately, that wound will not only leave an ugly scar but could also become infected, have irreparable damage, or be fatal. Sometimes the scars that we cannot see at first glance are the ones that hurt the most.

Fear is a feeling. If we allow ourselves to be consumed by the monster of fear, stress, and anxiety, we will be controlled by the monster. We cannot run, just cope with, hide, or ignore the monster in our lives, hoping that someday it will just go away.

If left unchallenged, the monster can take its toll and cause damage and wounds to a person's overall wellness.

Fear does not exist, but it does exist only in the minds of people who believe in it.

As people, we have the tendency to fear things that we do not understand or that we cannot control or predict the outcome. For example, a person who may not know much about dogs may be in fear if they are walking past a person who has a dog on a leash while someone who grew up with dogs or studied them due to their knowledge, wisdom, and understanding on the subject may feel in perfect peace when in the same situation.

Once we see ourselves differently, we will see the world differently.

It's time for us to clear the clutter out of our life so that we can make room for something brand-new! Let go of the negativity, anger, self-doubt, unforgiveness, stress, and fear.

When we attain a conqueror mindset, we will discover that we have the courage, confidence, and self-worth that will assist us in having the power to block or delete the number of that person who does not make us feel our very best on our phone.

Sometimes when people see a beautiful glass sculpture or vase, they fail to remember that the beautiful structure was once only sand. Only through undergoing over three thousand-degree temperature and process can that sand be transformed into a glass.

We are just like the sand, and only through pressure, perseverance, the process, and the test can we have a testimony as we transform into something brand-new. It is only through pressure that a diamond is formed. It is only going through the pressure and beating that a sword can reach its full potential and fulfill its purpose. It's only through the test that you can have a testimony. The only way to sharpen our blade is to apply a little bit of friction.

So if we feel that we had been through some things in the past or that we are going through some things right now, it is time for us to get excited because we are in the transformational process. We are all under construction and a work in progress. It is time for us to realize, that as a conqueror, what may have appeared to be an obstacle to the old version of ourselves, now arises to be an opportunity.

A conqueror knows that to conquer the monster in our lives no matter what form it presents itself it takes discipline, planning, consistency, the will to win, patience, action, humility, gratitude, and faith.

We have to be brave enough to create healthy boundaries for ourselves and others as long as they are established in love. A conqueror is a person who is strong enough to be honest with themselves. A conqueror shows mercy to others, is patient and humble, and values others.

Some people admire a butterfly, but they would not want to go through the transformational process that the caterpillar had to endure.

Other people admire the redwoods and the giant Sequoia trees that can live for thousands of years and stand hundreds of feet tall. Many people are not aware that in order for the pinecone to open up and release its seed, the pinecone had to go through fire and immense pressure that only it could endure. As we develop a conqueror mindset, we have to understand that only we could survive the situations that we went through. We are no longer just survivors; we are conquerors.

To be a conqueror, it takes discipline. That discipline will seem painful during the process, but after we put in the work, plow our field, and plant our seeds, in due season, we will have a beautiful harvest.

A conqueror understands that just a like diamond, oil, ruby, coal, and gold, we must dig in deep within ourselves to find the true value that is within. During this process, it will seem uncomfortable, but it will be rewarding in the end. We must realize that the monster will chase you only if you run.

Think about being in a nice warm bed at night, and you just found that comfortable spot. As you are warm in the blankets, you have a sudden urge to go use the bathroom. We now have a choice to make. We can either continue to lie in bed suffering from the discomfort and afraid that we are going to have an accident while waiting for our alarm clock to ring, or we can choose to be courageous and get out of the warm blankets and simply use the bathroom.

To have a conqueror mindset, a person has to understand that a conqueror is brave and knows that all things are possible if they believe. A conqueror understands the importance of journaling, writing things down, planning out their day in advance, having a vision, claiming victory, and maintaining a focus in reference to their desired goal.

A conqueror knows that every battle starts in their mind and learns to visualize their preferred outcome. A conqueror has integrity and does what is right even if it is not popular or comfortable. A conqueror consistently tests and trains their mind, body, and spirit. These disciplines are established through something called conqueror mindset challenges. These daily, weekly, monthly, and yearly challenges sharpen our sword and prepare us to be battle-tested and battle-ready for our victory.

A conqueror is willing to change and adapt in order to win. A conqueror is wise, humble, kind, and is receptive to coaching, guidance, and correction.

Like a sword, leaders are forged into greatness through adversity. It is time for us to sharpen our sword by having a conqueror mindset.

Leaders are made in adversity while managers and supervisors are positions and titles that are given by others.

A conqueror understands in communication, we have to connect before we become direct.

As we learn how to have a conqueror mindset, instead of running away from our fear, we will be courageous and face our fear, identify it, track it down, drag it into the light, and expose it for what it truly is. Once we have this monster of fear in the light, we can fully examine it. By looking at things objectively, we can gain knowledge, wisdom, and understanding in relation to this monster of fear.

We will never lose our eyesight by looking at things from a bright perspective, but we will always lose our focus when we stare into the fog.

A conqueror mindset assists us in understanding that everything is interconnected, depending on our perception and our perspective.

Everything in our life is based on our perception and our perspective. I have found that our perception and our perspective are influenced by our position. Our position is influenced by the angle from which we choose to see ourselves. How we see ourselves influences the way we see the world around us. Almost like looking in a mirror, we will reflect what we project. Similar to pointing our index finger at another person, if we look at our extended hand, we will see three fingers on our hand pointing back at us. We need to address the areas of weakness in our lives first, which will assist us in having the right energy filled with humility, grace, and patience when interacting with others. We will attract positive energy from others if we are positive. This can only occur if we walk in love. As we learn how to have a conqueror mindset, we will learn to be secure within who we really are so that we do not find ourselves becoming distracted or discouraged when faced with temptation, stress, fear, negative self-talk, and anxiety.

As we walk through the journey of life, we may stumble as we choose our own path. We can choose to live life allowing fear to dictate our past, present, and future; or we can choose to live life courageously and intentionally with expectancy as we conquer the monster of fear in our lives.

The only way to conquer the monster in our lives is to have a conqueror mindset. Once we humble ourselves and become honest with our feelings, we will be able to see more clearly and identify the monster in our lives. Let's stop overthinking, make a plan, take appropriate action, and know that we are more than conquerors, and conquer the monster.

Victory is waiting for us as soon as we find the courage to walk in it.

CHAPTER 8

CONQUER YOUR MONSTER

You are not your mother, father, sibling, or who you used to be in the past. You are not your job title or your position. You are one of the most valuable and powerful forces in the universe because you were made by the Creator. Let's not take the power of free will and responsibility of walking in love lightly. As we maintain a conqueror mindset, we will walk in humility, love, peace, and grace as we fully understand our values. We should wake up every day with an attitude of gratitude. Because you woke up today, every day is your birthday, and every day is a new year. Treat every day like it's a new beginning because tomorrow is never promised.

It's time to stop only talking about change and to start making that change happen. Let's live our life to its highest potential. Having a conqueror mindset teaches us that if we do not like our name, we have the power to change it; if we do not like our weight, car, hair, job, and so forth, we now have the power to change it.

Conquering the monster is a choice. It is time for us to choose to win this battle. The only reason why we have this bad habit or secret struggle is because of our current mindset. The beautiful thing about being a conqueror is that we have the power to say enough is enough. In every situation, we must ask ourselves, Is this helping me or hurting me?

We can choose to do our very best in all that we do and win.

Having a conqueror mindset is transformational. We will realize that we are eagles, and we do not have time to waste hanging around pigeons and ducks that flock together. We have the unique and rare ability to reach heights high above the clouds.

Having a conqueror mindset means that we have the ability to walk in truth. We can't continue to shoot ourselves in the foot and wonder why we are limping.

Freedom is found in truth, and once we identify our truth, we will be able to face any obstacle that has been hindering us from being free.

By having a conqueror mindset, we will begin to look at potential problems in your life as an equation. This way, we can find the proper formula for a solution.

A conqueror understands that a lion can beat a skunk any day of the week, but the question is, Is it really worth the stink?

Conquering the monster in our life is similar to hearing a noise in the back of the garage of our minds. As we walk deeper into the garage and lift a box only to find an aggressive raccoon or a large snake, what do we do? Do we just accept that it is there and do nothing, hoping that the raccoon or large snake does not have babies and make their way into our house, or do we adopt the conqueror mindset and identify the monster, make a plan in real time, and be courageous and take appropriate action that will finally give us freedom and peace of mind? We can't continue to hide underneath a blanket, hoping that the monster will just go away.

By having a conqueror mindset, I have learned that every anxiety and phobia is merely a fear of something, and every fear could be conquered simply by having greater knowledge, wisdom, and understanding of the fear and its source.

I remember working with a mental health professional on treatment teams. He was a nice person, but he had a bad habit of overcomplicating clients' treatments. After being introduced to a client who was afraid of dogs, within minutes, he would diagnose and slap a label on the client. Unfortunately, he was trained to treat symptoms instead of treating the root of the problem.

He was quick to issue and recommend pills, but he neglected to address the origin of the stimulus. If a person is afraid of dogs, instead of prescribing them a pill that may harm their kidneys, we could take the time to listen to the client and discover the origin of the fear; and after listening to the client, we could educate them in their area of concern eliminating their fear.

What good is it for us to continue to clip the leaves off the top of the weeds when we need to be courageous, dig deeper, and get to the root of the problem? We should not only focus on the fruit when the problem is coming from the root. Everything stems from the root.

We must remember that faith cannot exist without putting in the work. If we want a situation to change, we need to work toward that change. The conqueror mindset is more than an attitude and a mentality; it has to be real and part of who we are at the core.

Coping with fear is like accepting the fact that you have a small leak in the roof of your house that you refuse to fix. Everything seems fine, but it is only a matter of time before your ceiling collapses, also revealing mold. As we know, what we do in secret comes out to light. We can no longer be a hearer only; we must be a doer. We have the ability to dig deep within ourselves and encourage ourselves knowing that words are powerful, especially if backed with action.

Words are powerful.

A conqueror is a leader who is disciplined with their words, thoughts, and actions. Some people say that sticks and stones can break their bones, but words will never hurt them. A conqueror understands that words are powerful. Words can start fights between friends and family and wars between nations. Words can become a contributing factor toward people, harming, others or themselves.

A conqueror understands that we cannot be in the business of punishing people. A conqueror knows the value of forgiveness. We must be able to forgive ourselves so that we can be able to forgive others. As we develop a conqueror mindset, we will discover that life and death are in the power of our tongue. When having a conqueror mindset, we will know that a ten-second comment can destroy a twenty-year career and tarnish what once was a positive reputation.

A conqueror realizes that not every comment needs a response, and not every action needs a reaction.

We must continue to realize that every day is a battle, and we need to walk with expectancy, joy, peace, faithfulness, and in the confidence knowing that we have already won. Doing this will allow us to walk through life stress-free and with the right energy.

We have to remember that energy cannot be created nor destroyed, but it can only be transferred from one object to another. It's time to manifest the greatness that is already inside of us. With a conqueror mindset, we will realize that we need to model the way as well as the behavior that we would like to see in others. A conqueror is intelligent, strong, skilled, humble, and like a bright city on top of a hill. It is also like a bright light in a room full of darkness.

The enemy wants us to hold onto fear, unforgiveness, anger, and hatred. We will conquer the monster in our life by addressing what makes us feel uncomfortable.

It is time for us to let go of everything that is toxic in our lives. It is time to let go of toxic people, food, thoughts, behaviors, and habits as we cleanse ourselves from negativity. It is time for us to break down the walls, barriers, and obstructions in our lives that have been hindering and distracting us. We can avoid the land mines in life if we are willing to look at situations from an objective point of view.

As we develop a conqueror mindset, we will know that the monster of fear is at the root of suffering. Fear is the threat of harm; this potential harm can be real or imagined. If we feel uncomfortable or unpleasant about something, this feeling is rooted in fear. Fear is an emotion that arises when danger is perceived.

By using the conqueror, mindset principle, we will realize that fear, stress, phobia, and anxiety are all based on the way we think, which is influenced by our perception. We will see molehills or mountains depending on the lens we choose to look through. Are we afraid and full of anxiety speaking in public or walking in front of a crowd, or are we excited? Our heart rate may increase as our senses will become more alert; the only difference is our state of mind.

In order to affect change in our lives, we need to do something different.

Every person is different. We all have our own past experiences, perceptions, and perspectives on life. This one-size-fits-all approach to mental health is not working. We must stop hiding behind titles and accolades, slapping Band-Aids on serious wounds only to later wonder why there is an infection. When interacting with people, we must meet them where they are and realize that behind their current circumstances is a real person in need. Every person is going through something at some level. We need to be respectful as we understand that we are all under construction and a work in progress.

When faced with a monster and its many forms, a conqueror understands the difference between reacting to a stimuli and responding to one. Reacting means to meet one action with another. We usually do this without thinking clearly or when we are in an irrational state of mind. When responding, we must remember that this word derives from the word *responsibility*, and it is deliberate, thought-out, and intentional. From this point on, we need to learn how to respond to people and circumstances rather than react to them. The monster will always attempt to get a reaction out of us. We need to stop reacting and start responding.

A conqueror understands that having self-love is not selfish. When having a conqueror mindset, we will understand that the monster will always say the quiet part out loud hoping that we are not listening. We can no longer suffer in silence drowning while being too afraid, ashamed, prideful, or embarrassed to raise our hand to ask for help.

Conquerors know that their mental health is their greatest wealth, and their self-worth is more valuable than their net worth. A conqueror has a strong will, a loving heart, and an attitude of gratitude with a mindset that will never be defeated.

Some people have the tendency to look away from what makes them feel uncomfortable. A conqueror is willing to fight fiction with facts and turn fear into power. It is time for us to be courageous, invest in ourselves, and do the best that we can do in all that we do.

Let's stay inspired as we put in the hard work and live life intentionally with expectancy while maintaining a conqueror mindset. Let's continue to be quick to listen, slow to speak, be bold as a lion as we walk in love and conquer the monster in our lives.

ACKNOWLEDGMENTS

I must start by thanking my amazing wife, Erica Dannielle. Thank you for being in my opinion the most magnificent woman in the world. I love you and cannot thank you enough for holding down the fort as I spent time in my office writing. There are no words that can fully describe just how incredible you are. You were as important to this book getting done as I was. Thank you for all your love, support, and patience when I was assigned to special missions, operations, projects, and assignments over the years. Thank you so much for being someone who I trust, love, respect, and admire. You have a conqueror mindset. You are highly intelligent, strong, patient, kind, and simply magnificent in every way possible! You are the strongest and most beautiful person I know. Thank you for being such a wonderful mother to our son. Thank you for being an extraordinary wife and best friend! You are beautiful internally and externally! You are truly a noblewoman, and I thank God for you daily! I love you, always and forever!

A special thank you to my son Michael Alexander the Great, who is highly intelligent and one of the most creative minds that I have ever seen. You have a conqueror mindset and a conqueror mentality. I can't thank you enough for your patience and input while I was writing this book. You are wise beyond your years and one of the smartest people on the planet. Your talent and skill level are simply unmatched. When I think about you, the only word that comes to mind is *greatness*! You are a prudent man and brilliant. Thank you for catching the spelling errors in my notes and drafts in this book before I did. I feel as if I am the happiest and most blessed person in the world because I have you for a son. You're the best son that any dad could ask for! Thank you for being one of the most incredible people on the planet. You are a real-life superhero! I love you with all my heart!

I want to thank my mother, father, siblings, in-laws, and every member of the Roberts, Perez, Genwright, and Horton families for all their love and support throughout the years that helped make this book possible. There are no words that can fully describe how I feel about you all! God bless you always, and thank you again for everything!

Elliott Genwright, a special thank you for all your incredible insight, love, and support throughout the years which helped make this book possible. Thank you for your continued service to others and for being a blessing. Thank you for helping me assist people in understanding that they are bigger than the monster that they are facing. You are an amazing dad to your remarkable daughter and an awesome husband to your beautiful and brilliant wife. You are highly intelligent and insightful. You are a great leader and a true gift from God.

Emily Thomas, I just wanted to thank you for being an amazing person. You and your family are incredible. Any person who is blessed to interact with you is fortunate. You are the best in your field. You are very creative, resourceful, and intelligent. I want to thank you for helping me assist people around the world. You are a true godsend. You are blessed with amazing gifts and talents. Thank you for all that you do behind the scenes.

Cherie Johnson, thank you for being such a wonderful person! You have one of the most creative minds in the universe. You are an extraordinary inventor, creator, and world changer. Thank you for helping me assist people around the world in overcoming and conquering anything in their life that is holding them back from being their very best. It's time for us to step outside of our comfort zone. Thank you for being such an incredible person. I love you and your family always. I am still your big brother! Thank you for all of your love and support over the years. Your skillset is limitless. Thank you for being all that you are. You are a gift to the world!

Torri Strickland, you are 2222 amazing!! You are a magnificent person that is highly intelligent, loving, creative, insightful, and a conqueror. I can't thank you enough for your love, wisdom, expertise, leadership, and support. Thank you for helping me uplift and encourage others to never give up!! Thank you for helping me assist people in overcoming the monster in their life and realizing that on the other side of fear are peace and freedom!! You are very passionate, a go-getter, and a true blessing to the world!! Thank you for being the best in the business. You have one of the kindest hearts and strongest minds that I have ever seen! Thank you for being incredible!! Love to you and your wonderful family!!

Jessica Knoll, thank you for having a wonderful heart, positive disposition, and creative mind! Thank you for helping me inspire others while assisting me in spreading a message of hope, joy, and love to people around the world! Thank you for assisting me in helping others to look at things from a bright perspective. Thank you for your assistance in supporting my goal to help people in overcoming and conquering the monster of stress, fear, addiction, and anxiety. I admire and love your dedication to being a blessing to your family and the way you serve others with a giving heart. Thank you for being amazing!

Bill Bevins, thank you for having such a great personality and assisting me in helping people overcome negative self-talk and self-doubt. Thank you for assisting me in helping others realize that by changing the way we see things, the way we think, and the way we speak, we can assist them in living a life with less stress, fear, and anxiety.

Evanne Armour, thank you for helping me assist people in realizing that we need to walk in love and pause before speaking and making decisions that may be life altering. Thank you for assisting me in spreading a message of joy while teaching people that it's not about thinking outside of the box; it's about realizing that there is no box for us to think outside of in the first place.

Frances Peyton, I can't thank you enough for all that you have done for me. You are a perfect combination of strength, intelligence, and love! Thank you for assisting me in uplifting people around the world. Thank you for helping me assist people in realizing that the fight doesn't go to the swift or the strong but to the one who can endure until the end. You are insightful, and I can't thank you enough for all of your amazing efforts behind the scenes! Thank you for being a true gift from God to the world!

Thank you to every member of *Virginia This Morning* family, cast, and crew. Thank you for helping me motivate, encourage, and inspire people to never give up despite their circumstances or situation.

A special thank you to the CBS 6 family, its leadership, and all staff members. Thank you to every film and sound technician as well as every anchor and reporter. Without all your love and support, this book would not be possible. You all are amazing!

Special thank you to NBC 12 news, its leadership as well as every staff member. You all have been extraordinary in assisting me and helping people around the world overcome stress, fear, and anxiety. Without all your support, this book would not be possible!

A. J. Nwoko, I can't thank you enough for being one of the most detailed and creative people that I have ever met! Because of your vision, you have helped change the lives of millions of people for the better! I can't thank you enough for your expertise, professionalism, and assistance and for making it possible for this book to reach millions of people around the world! Thank you for all your hard work, love, and support! You are one of the best journalists and video creators on the planet! Thank you for being a true shining star! None of this would be possible without you!

Patricia Avila, a.k.a. "Paty the Superhero," I can't thank you enough for being who you are and for what you represent! You are an amazing friend and an extraordinary gift to the world! Thank you for assisting me in helping people around the world to overcome and conquer negative stimuli that are holding them back from being their very best! Thank you for assisting me in helping people develop a better mind, body, and spirit. You are the very best at what you do! You are a true superhero with a loving heart. Thank you for being incredible!

Thank you to the entire cast and crew of 757 and We are Living Healthy for helping me spread a message of joy, inspiration, and love to people around the world!

Melissa Hewitt, thank you for your expertise. You are smarter than a supercomputer! Thank you for your technical support and intelligence. Thank you for assisting me to have a platform and for helping me reach millions of people around the world. I can't thank you enough for all the work that you do behind the scenes! You are a wonderful person!

Ashley Snyder thank you for having a great heart and for assisting me in inspiring others to realize that their perception of things does not have to be their reality. We have the power to take action and change our circumstances. You are one of a kind!

Will Rodriguez, thank you for all your support and for not being afraid to challenge the status quo.

Alexis Perkins, thank you for helping me spread a message of faith and hope to the world. You are a go-getter who is intelligent, and you have a beautiful heart! Thank you for helping me teach others to continue to be quick to listen, slow to speak, and to walk in love.

Quincy Carr, thank you for being one of the funniest men on the planet and for using your gifts and abilities to assist me in uplifting and encouraging others to never give up! You are a wonderful father and a great person!

Richmond Family Magazine, thank you to the leadership and every staff member for your support and for assisting me in spreading a message of faith, hope, and love that conquers all. I can't thank you enough for all that you have done for me and for making this book possible! Thank you for assisting me in spreading a message of hope to others. Thank you to the leadership as well as every staff member. You all are amazing!

Joan Tupponce, thank you for all your love and support! You are highly skilled, and you have a creative mind! I can't thank you enough for all that you have done in making this book possible! Thank you for assisting me in encouraging people to never give up despite any circumstance!

Liberty University, thank you for being, in my humble opinion, one of the best universities in the country! Thank you to all the staff members, students, alumni, and leadership for making this world a better place and for preparing leaders for excellence!

Nina Vires, thank you for being one of the brightest minds and purest hearts. You are highly intelligent and insightful! Thank you for helping me assist people in overcoming limiting beliefs and for them to know all things are possible if we believe!

Jacob Couch, thank you for being the wonderful person that you are! Thank you for assisting me in encouraging people to know that sometimes we will be faced with extreme adversity in the form of a monster, and instead of running from it, we need to run toward it which will surprise and confuse the enemy. Thank you for helping me assist people to overcome illness, stress, fear, and anxiety.

Wedding Chicks, you are the very best in the business. Thank you for assisting me in uplifting, motivating, and encouraging people around the world. You all are amazing people.

Amy Zawacki, thank you for being such a go-getter and for having a beautiful heart! Thank you for helping me assist people in overcoming stress, fear, anxiety, self-sabotage, and negative self-talk! Thank you for helping me show people that words are powerful and that we need to choose to speak life over ourselves as we walk and love! Thank you for helping me teach people that we need to replace the word *sorry* with the word *thank you.* Instead of saying, "Sorry for being late," we now will say, "Thank you for your patience." You are an amazing person!

Thank you, *Love What Matters*, for assisting me in encouraging people to never give up despite any situation or circumstance.

Sofia San Filippo, thank you for helping me make this book possible and for assisting me in reaching people around the world with a message of hope and perseverance. You are highly intelligent, and you have a great heart. Thank you for all your love and support.

Thank you, Waylon Lewis, you are highly intelligent and a go-getter. Thank you for being a true blessing to so many people.

Elephant Journal, thank you for helping me teach others to be courageous enough to seek self-awareness. Thank you for assisting me in my mission to inspire, motivate, and encourage others to love one another as they seek mindfulness.

Katie Fleming, thank you for helping me spread love, joy, and mindfulness to people around the world. Thank you for assisting me in teaching people that it's not about the *you* and *I* but rather the *we* and *us*. Without you, this book would not be possible.

Robert Busch, thank you for helping me reach millions of people around the world by spreading a message of love, joy, and peace. Thank you for helping me teach people that if two people see a spider web, one may see the beauty and creativity of the web while someone else, depending on their mindset and past experience, may see a death trap that houses a dangerous predator that is ready to devour potential prey. Life is all about our perception and our perspective. You are an incredible person.

Shawn Freude, you are a true genius, and I can't thank you enough for all that you do behind the scenes! You truly have assisted me in reaching a broader audience in my quest to help people overcome negative stimuli. Thank you for having an intelligent mind and a loving heart.

Louise Keeton, thank you for making this book possible and assisting me in reaching people around the world! You are driven, and you have a great heart! Thank you again for all that you do!

Christian Faith Publishing, thank you for all that you do to make this world a better place! Thank you to all the editors, proofreaders, design team, cover team, and every staff member for allowing this book to reach people around the world and affect positive change in their lives. I am thankful for all your love and support. Thank you to all the CFP family for all your love and support. Thank you for assisting me in spreading a message of faith, joy, love, and determination. Thank you to the entire staff and leadership for being a true blessing!

Lisa Bolen, thank you for all your insight and wisdom! You have been a tremendous asset. Thank you for being such an extraordinary person with a wonderful heart! God bless you and your family always! Without your assistance, this book would not be possible. Thank you for helping me reach and assist people around the world in personal development and coaching.

Shannon Cherpak, thank you for assisting me in making this possible! Thank you for helping me reach people around the world and for helping me inspire them to never give up as they conquer stress, fear, and anxiety in their life. You have a great personality, disposition, and mindset. You are blessed with intelligence, beauty, and strength. Thank you for being such an incredible person!

Bobbi Bryant and Bobbi Bryant modeling, thank you for being in my humble opinion one of the best photographers in the country! Without you, this book would not be possible, and I can't thank you enough for all your contributions, support, and love!

Carol Adams and the Carol Adams Foundation. Thank you, Carol, for all that you do for others. You are a blessing to the world. Thank you for giving me a platform and for helping me assist people to overcome and conquer the monster in their lives. You are simply magnificent!

Ilene Carol and *Women's Quarterly Magazine, New League Magazine,* and Extended Hugs Charity. Ilene, thank you for your love and support by assisting me in uplifting, encouraging, and inspiring others. You are the best at what you do.

Thank you to the Honorable Sheriff Vanessa Crawford. Thank you for continually assisting me in uplifting, motivating, and inspiring others. Your work is legendary. Thank you for helping me assist people in overcoming and conquering the monsters in their lives. You are a true gift from God.

Judith Simpson, you are an absolute joy and blessing! Thank you so much for being a true gift from God and a blessing to the world! Thank you for all your love and support which helped make this book possible! I couldn't have done any of this without your assistance and support!

Christian L. Simson, you are one of the brightest minds that this world has ever seen! Anyone associated with you is truly blessed. Thank you so much for being such a wonderful person and for all your love and support since the beginning of this entire process!

Elliott Anderson, you are one of the most intelligent people on the planet! I can't thank you enough for your wisdom and diligence in helping others! Thank you for all your love and support! Without you, this book would not be possible! Throughout the years you have continued to show that you are an amazing person with a great heart!

Beatrice Anderson, you have been one of the biggest blessings to my family and me! Thank you for all that you do behind the scenes. You are a true blessing from heaven and a godsend to the world! Thank you for your years of service to others. Thank you so much for your extraordinary knowledge, wisdom, and grace!

Thank you to all the courageous men, women, and children in the world who are bold enough to stand up to monsters, bullies, thugs, hate groups, gangs, terrorists, dictators, tyrants, abusers, manipulators, con men, injustice, and criminals.

Thank you to all the men and women who stand up for what is right and run toward danger to save others. Thank you to all first responders who risk their lives to be a blessing to others. Thank you to every person who does the job the right way with integrity, bravery, morality, courage, and professionalism. Thank you to every person who stands in the gap even when it is not popular and who is willing to act rather than be frozen by fear. Thank you for being that thin line between peace and chaos, life and death, good and evil.

Thank you to every federal, state, regional, county, city, private agency, bureau, department, business, corporation, and office that I had the honor and pleasure to work with. Thank you to every supervisor, coach, trainer, mentor, and coworker who I had the honor to learn from and work with.

Thank you to every member of the media for assisting me in my purpose to bring awareness to mental health and for assisting me in helping people around the world overcome and conquer stress, fear, and anxiety in their lives.

Most importantly, I would like to thank God. Thank you, for being the source of my strength and for giving me knowledge, wisdom, and understanding. Thank you for allowing me to have the opportunity to honor you and remind people that they are stronger than their circumstances. Thank you for helping me assist people around the world in becoming their best selves and realizing that they are more than a conqueror. Thank you for the extraordinary people that you have placed in my life to make this book possible.

ABOUT THE AUTHOR

Robert Conqueror Roberts is dedicated and has a unique ability in helping people everywhere create a life they love by following their dreams and achieving their biggest goals by identifying, confronting, and conquering fear. Rob is the creator of the Conqueror Mindset.

He is an award-winning personal development expert, author, speaker, certified life coach, personal trainer, and self-defense instructor, with over three decades of experience.

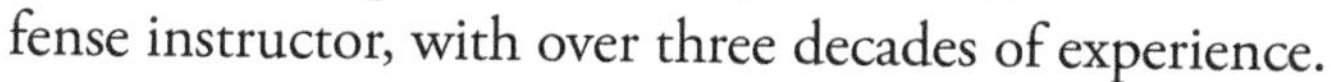

Rob is a former college football player and scholar-athlete, who has received several academic awards and honors. He has a degree in criminal justice from Liberty University. Rob is a published writer and photographer, entrepreneur, and former award-winning federal law enforcement officer. He has been featured in television commercials, films, movies, talk shows, radio, magazines, and other social media platforms.

He has received numerous honors, accommodations, and awards in mental health, intelligence, coaching, business, fitness, martial arts, and counseling for children and adults. Rob is a former executive team member and department head for government and private agencies. He is a former corporate trainer, counselor, corporate detective, and intelligence officer. Rob has worked for numerous specialized tactical, investigative, surveillance, emergency response, and intelligence units.

Rob gives a new perspective and perception on obtaining self-awareness and mindfulness. Instead of teaching people how to cope with the monster of negative stimuli, he teaches how to have the capacity to overcome and conquer the monster.

Rob is happily married to the love of his life, Erica Dannielle, and is the proud father to their incredible son, Michael.

Printed in the USA
CPSIA information can be obtained
at www.ICGtesting.com
LVHW040558261123
764762LV00053B/1666